The Director's guide to accounting and finance

Other books by **M. G. Wright** published by McGRAW-HILL
Discounted Cash Flow (second edn)
Financial Management
Case Studies in Financial Management

The Director's guide to accounting and finance

M.G.Wright, B. Com., FCCA, FCIS

Principal Lecturer, School of Management,
Polytechnic of Central London
Consultant, Whitehead Consulting Group, London

McGRAW-HILL Book Company (UK) Limited

London · New York · St Louis · San Francisco · Auckland · Bogotá
Düsseldorf · Johannesburg · Madrid · Mexico · Montreal · New Delhi
Panama · Paris · São Paulo · Singapore · Sydney · Tokyo · Toronto

Published by

McGRAW-HILL Book Company (UK) Limited
MAIDENHEAD · BERKSHIRE · ENGLAND

Library of Congress Cataloging in Publication Data

Wright, Maurice Gordon.
    The director's guide to accounting and finance.

    Includes index.
    1. Corporations—Finance. 2. Corporations—Accounting. I.   Title.
HG4026.W68   658.1'5   76-26625
ISBN 0-07-084479-8

1 2 3 4 5 APL 7 9 8 7 6

Printed and bound in Great Britain

To my family—for their forebearance

Contents

Preface

The successful management of a company depends upon the directors having, in addition to their technical and other skills, a grasp of the working of the financial function and an understanding of how financial information is used in decision making. Simply because an executive has been highly successful in his particular specialism is no guarantee that he will be successful as a director. The role of a director is much wider than that of a functional executive and requires a balance of skills, both within the individual director and within the board of directors itself.

The duties of a director, moreover, require him, whatever his technical training, to assume certain responsibilities for the accounting and reporting function. Some of these obligations are laid down by statute and failure to observe such requirements can bring legal penalties on the directors. Other requirements, while not laid down by statute, may bring censure on the directors if not observed. The director should have a clear idea what these responsibilities are so that he can ensure that his company does not default on any requirements.

In addition to statutory and other requirements for the disclosure of information and record keeping, directors need to understand how management actions are reflected in the performance of the company and what they need to do to effectively plan and control the activities of the companies that they manage. Much of this planning and control is expressed in financial terms and the director must be in a position to communicate with accountants and others in their own language.

Ultimately the survival of the company will depend upon the ability of the board of directors to develop the right balance in the sources of funds used to finance the company and the way in which those funds are employed. Planning and control in this area is vital if the company is to continue to be able to fulfil its obligations to others. It is an area, however, where the problems of planning and control are exacerbated by rampant inflation and the implications of inflation for company finance and profit measurement should be clearly understood.

This book is designed to provide directors with the basic knowledge of the accounting requirements and those of financial report disclosure; with information that they require to perform their duties, such as the tax structure and sources of capital; with the ability to analyse performance; and to provide a statement of their roles in planning and decision taking and the control process.

Welwyn   M.G.WRIGHT
January 1976

1.

The financial report

It is often felt that the annual financial report is a rather arid document prepared by accountants and only interpretable by accountants. This should not be so. It is a report by management of their stewardship of the business during the past year (or other period) to the shareholders. As such, it is the financial expression of the outcome of management actions and decisions related to the economic conditions of the period, in so far as they have affected assets and obligations of the business and its income, and how that income is to be appropriated.

Every management decision will affect the financial report in some way and it represents an attempt to analyse and synthesize those effects in a manner which will enable people who read the report to gain an understanding of what has happened in general terms. Normally, of course, the outcome of individual actions is not shown in the report—they are lost in the aggregate effect of all the actions during the period. Sometimes, however, the effect of individual actions must be shown, such as when a major investment becomes unprofitable and is disposed of at a loss.

The financial report should, therefore, show how well the directors have husbanded the assets and used the resources of the company to generate income.

Who uses it?

Since the directors are stewards managing the affairs of the company on behalf of its owners—the shareholders—the financial report is primarily a stewardship report to the shareholders. In reading the report they will be trying to form a view as to the strength of the company, its profitability, stability and potential for long-term growth, and the possibility of being called upon to provide more funds to support the company's operations. In forming such a view they may well also form a view as to the quality of the management of the company.

In their presentation of the financial report the directors should appreciate that among the shareholders are numbered both the sophisticated analyst and the private investor who has no financial knowledge at all. If the financial report is to perform its function of communicating information it must be presented in a style that is comprehensible to all shades of financial sophistication. Accounting jargon should be avoided and items in the report described in a manner which is most likely to be understood by the layman.

Other people will also be interested in reading the report. Potential future shareholders will use it as part of the data on which they decide whether or not to invest in the company. Creditors may use it to decide whether or not to extend further credit to the company, as may bank managers in deciding on overdraft facilities. The tax liability of the company will also be based upon the same data as that included in the accounts (but see chapter 4).

Normally one would expect the users mentioned above to employ suitably qualified people who are capable of interpreting the accounts in the light of their own particular requirements. The other group that may use the report will not, however, have that sophistication. This is the case where the report is made available to employees. This is a growing practice and one which, in the current social climate, is likely to become prevalent. To ensure that the report is fully understood it may be more desirable to prepare a separate statement based on the accounts included in the report and present it in narrative or pictorial form most likely to be understood by the recipients.

What does it consist of?

The Companies Acts 1948 and 1967 formalize the period for reporting and the minimum contents of the report. These require that a report be laid before the company in general meeting at least once in every year. Occasionally the length of the accounting period may be varied for a number of reasons, such as a take-over of another company with a different accounting date, but normally it will be an annual event.

The report consists of three main parts:
1. The balance sheet.
2. The profit and loss account.
3. The directors' report.

In addition there must be attached to every set of accounts laid before the company an auditor's report on them. Holding companies also have to submit group accounts in addition to their own.

The balance sheet is a statement of affairs at one particular point in time—the end of the financial year. As such it sets out the assets and liabilities and other obligations of the business at that date. The profit and loss account is a statement of how the income for the period has been earned and what is proposed for its appropriation. The full detailed profit and loss account is not usually published, as it could provide vital information to competitors.

Only that information which is required to be disclosed is usually included.

The directors have the prime responsibility for the manner in which the annual report is presented. The Companies Acts do not specify any particular format but confine themselves to establishing minimum disclosure requirements which are dealt with in the next chapter. The only overriding requirement is that they should show a 'true and fair' view of the state of affairs at the balance sheet date and of the profit for the year ended on that date. To achieve this they should be presented in accordance with generally accepted accounting practice applied on a consistent basis. The process of defining generally accepted accounting practice has proceeded in recent years under the authority of a body called the Accounting Standards Committee on which are represented all the major accounting bodies.

The ASC has already established a number of statements of standard accounting practices (SSAPs). All members of the accountancy bodies are expected to follow these SSAPs in presenting accounts, and where appropriate to urge their boards of directors to do so. If a company does not follow the SSAP in a particular respect then it is likely that the audit certificate would carry a report to that effect. However, although there are a number of external constraints on the preparation and presentation of the financial report, it is the report of the directors and they are entirely responsible for it.

Nature and composition of the balance sheet

The balance sheet is made of four basic building blocks as shown below:

Balance sheet of X Ltd as at 31.12.75

| Long-term funds | Fixed assets |
| Current liabilities | Current assets |

If arranged in a two-sided presentation, such as that illustrated above, the two sides of the balance sheet should agree. This is not accountant's 'magic' but reflects the fact that each transaction of the company has two opposing effects in the accounts—what the accountant is basically referring to when he talks about double entry book-keeping. For example, if the company pays £10 000 corporation tax to the Inland Revenue, that transaction reduces the company's cash resources by that amount and reduces its liability for tax by the same amount.

The accounting system summarizes these two effects for all transactions during the period in accounts which record various items of income or expenditure and assets and liabilities. The balance sheet and profit and loss account are built up from the balances of such accounts suitably adjusted for outstanding items.

The fixed asset block consists of long-term assets, such as buildings, plant and machinery, equipment, and vehicles. Also included would be long-term investments in other companies, and goodwill. Fixed assets are necessary for the continuance of the company's business and are not purchased with the primary intention of resale at a profit (that may happen, but it is subsidiary to the main purpose).

Current assets are short-term assets, such as stocks and work in progress (or inventory) and debtors (or accounts receivable), which are held for the short-term conversion into cash and in the process generate the trading profits, together with cash itself. Whether or not an asset is fixed or current depends upon the *purpose* for which it is held and not its physical nature, e.g., although land is usually a fixed asset, if it is held by a house builder for development and resale after houses have been erected it is a current asset. Sometimes assets may not be easily distinguished between fixed and current and they should appear between the two blocks.

Current liabilities are those liabilities which the company can be called upon to pay within the 12 months following the balance sheet date. It includes such items as creditors, bank overdrafts, taxation and dividends. Further, if a long-term loan falls due for payment within that period it should also be included in this block.

Long-term funds comprise all the funds committed to the business on a long-term basis, whether by the shareholders or lenders of money.

The shareholders' funds comprise the amounts subscribed by shareholders for shares in the company and undistributed profits and gains. Gains other than from normal trading activities may appear as capital reserves, and would include such items as surpluses arising from the revaluation of assets, sales of fixed assets at a profit, less exceptional losses. Undistributed profits from normal trading operations, such as the balance on the profit and loss account, should appear as revenue reserves. Long-term loans include mortgages, debentures, and secured and unsecured loans. They represent money which the company is committed to repaying at specific dates and on which it must pay interest.

Also included in long-term funds may be items where there is a deferred payment, e.g., deferred taxation.

Function of the balance sheet

The function of the balance sheet is to show how the business has been financed and how the funds raised are being employed. How the business is financed is shown by the long-term funds block of the balance sheet, and of particular concern here, as will be explored later, is the balance between shareholders' funds and money which the company has borrowed. The employment of funds is shown by the total of fixed and current assets less current liabilities—a net value usually described as 'net assets'.

The modern balance sheet presentation usually reflects these two functions by rearranging the four blocks in one of the following ways:

	Method A		Method B

Uses of funds: (Method A)   *Uses of funds:* (Method B)

	Method A		Method B
	Fixed assets		Fixed assets
Plus:	Current assets	*Plus:*	
	————		Current assets
=	Total assets		
		Less: Current liabilities	
Less:	Current liabilities	————	
	————	=	Working capital
=	Net assets		————
	════	=	Net assets
			════
Financed by:	Long-term funds	*Financed by:*	Long-term funds
	════		════

A typical balance sheet presentation is that shown for X Ltd in Table 1.1.

TABLE 1.1
Balance sheet of X Ltd
Balance sheet of X Ltd as at 31 December 1975

Uses of funds
Fixed assets: (£000s)

Land and buildings		2068
Plant and equipment		2322
		4390
Goodwill		925
Current assets:		
Stocks and work in progress	1971	
Debtors and payments in advance	1201	
Balances at banks and cash in hand	138	
		3310
		8625
Less:		
Current liabilities:		
Trade creditors and accrued charges	563	
Bank overdrafts (secured)	492	
Taxation	357	
Final dividend	203	
		1615
NET ASSETS		7010
Financed by		
Shareholder's funds:		
Authorized share capital:		
8 000 000 ordinary shares of 25p each		2000

TABLE 1.1 (*cont.*)

Issued share capital:	
7 740 000 ordinary shares of 25p each	1935
Reserves	3847
	5782
Secured loans	1097
Deferred taxation	131
	7010

The profit and loss account

As already stated, the financial report usually only contains certain minimum information and not the full profit and loss account. This minimum consists of:

1. Turnover for the year.
2. The trading profit for the year together with details of those items charged in arriving at that profit which by law must be disclosed.
3. Non-trading income and expenditure.
4. Taxation.
5. The amount of profits after tax which are to be distributed as dividends and retained in the company.

TABLE 1.2

Profit and loss account of X Ltd

Profit and loss account for X Limited for the year to 31 December 1975

		£000s
Turnover		7226
Net profit for the year[1]		1109
Taxation based upon the profit for the year:		
Corporation tax	340	
Less:		
Double taxation relief	104	
	236	
Overseas taxation	269	
	—	505
Net profit after taxation		604
Less:		
Interim dividend (net)	135	
Final dividend (net)	203	
	—	338
Profits for the year retained in the business		266

[1] Certain items charged against profit in arriving at this figure must be disclosed.

A typical profit and loss account included in the annual report is that shown in Table 1.2.

Group accounts

Where a company has subsidiary companies (i.e., companies of which broadly it owns over 50 per cent of the shares) it must publish in addition to its own balance sheet and profit and loss account a group or consolidated balance sheet and profit and loss account. The objective of the group accounts is to show the state of affairs and the profit of the group as a single entity.

The group balance sheet is compiled by aggregating the assets and liabilities (other than shareholders' funds) of all the companies in the group, including the parent, with the totals adjusted for inter-company balances and holdings. This process will be facilitated if uniform accounting policies are adopted by each company and there is a common year end date. Usually a single profit and loss account is presented for both the company and the group. This shows the details outlined above for the profit and loss account for the whole group up to the profit after tax stage. From the profit after tax is then deducted that proportion of profits in subsidiary companies which are owned by outside shareholders in those subsidiaries, and the retained profit is divided between that held by the parent and that held by subsidiaries.

Inter-company profits

The group cannot make a profit by trading between its constituent members. Therefore, in the group accounts the turnover shown represents only sales to third parties, and the profit element in stocks of goods purchased from other group companies must be eliminated.

Minority interests

The group as a whole is financed by the long-term funds of the parent company and that part of the long-term funds of each subsidiary which are held by outside parties. That part of the total shareholders' funds of subsidiary companies which the parent does not own can be aggregated and shown as a single item in the long-term funds block of the group balance sheet as 'minority interests', or some similar descriptive title.

Goodwill

When the company acquires a new subsidiary company it is in fact acquiring the net assets of that subsidiary that are attributable to the shares that it acquires. The price that it pays for the shares acquired may be greater or less than that net asset value. If it is greater, the difference is shown as 'goodwill', 'premium on acquisition of shares in subsidiary companies' or some similar title. If it is less than the surplus value of net assets it is added to capital reserve.

The following illustrates the acquisition of a company with net assets of £10 000 where the parent holds 75 per cent of the subsidiary's share capital and outside shareholders continue to own 25 per cent:

	£
Total net attributable assets	10 000
Less: ¼ minority interest	2 500
Value of net assets attributable to parent company	7 500
Cost of acquisition	9 000
Goodwill	1 500

The total net assets are aggregated with those of other group companies in the group balance sheet, goodwill will be shown as an asset in the group balance sheet, the minority interest will form part of the group long-term funds, and the net of those values (£9000) offsets the cost of acquiring the subsidiary company as shown in the parent company's books.

It is quite common to write off goodwill against capital reserve on the grounds that it is an intangible asset. Before doing so, however, the directors should consider the implications of this practice for the measurements of profitability that will be discussed later.

Pre-acquisition profits

That part of a subsidiary company's undistributed profits that were earned before the company became a subsidiary have been purchased by the parent through the outlay of some of its capital. They are not, therefore, available for distribution to the parent company's shareholders. Only profits earned by the subsidiary after it becomes a subsidiary are so available.

Valuation problems

Accounts are often misunderstood by their readers as it is believed that the accountant is able to put precise values on assets and that those assets could be realized if need be and turned into cash at the book values. In fact, asset values in the accounts are based upon people's judgement of what those values are. The exercise of this judgement is primarily the responsibility of the directors. While other people's experience may be called upon in the process of valuation, in the end the directors must bear the responsibility.

Examples of the judgement values required are those related to depreciation, the valuation of stocks and work in progress, and provisions for bad debts. At the balance sheet date only the cost of a fixed asset is known, together with the period of time it has been owned so far. What is not known is how much longer the company will own the asset or what it will realize when it is eventually sold. Stocks of materials or goods may prove to be slow moving, may deteriorate or become obsolete, and this must be allowed for in their valuation; not all the amounts owing to the company at the balance sheet date may be collectable as people may go bankrupt or companies go into liquidation, or for other reasons. Some allowance must be made for this in determining the value which is to appear in the balance sheet.

The directors should set the guidelines that are to be used in this process of valuation and assure themselves that those guidelines are being adhered to by those to whom the detail of the valuation is entrusted.

The role of the auditor

The auditors are appointed by the shareholders at the annual general meeting to examine the accounts submitted by the directors and report on them to the shareholders. Because of the close relationship that must exist between the directors and the auditor, it is often felt that they are appointed by and are responsible to the board, and indeed in most cases it is the directors who recommend the appointment to the shareholders.

The auditors are, however, completely independent of the board and will guard that independence jealously. They may, in fact, sometimes be in conflict with the directors over the accounting treatment of certain items in the accounts. If such a conflict cannot be resolved to the satisfaction of the auditor then he may feel obliged to qualify his report to the shareholders in respect of that item. This does not necessarily indicate that there is anything wrong with the accounts, but only that in the view of the auditor a matter, such as the way a particular asset is valued, does not accord with his view. But his view of the matter and the directors' can both be honestly held. They are merely exercising their judgement in different ways.

2.

Statutory and other responsibilities for books and records

Accounting information is principally used to provide the basis for a wide range of management planning and decision taking and should be structured with those needs in mind. However, the basic accounting records and the financial report to the shareholders must conform to certain standards of disclosure laid down in the Companies Acts and to standards of disclosure and practice provided for by extra-statutory bodies, such as the Accounting Standards Committee and the stock exchange. The directors are responsible for ensuring that the company satisfies such requirements, and they may personally incur the penalties laid down in the Acts for non-compliance with the statutory requirements. Non-compliance with other requirements may mean that the company's accounts may be qualified by the auditor or the company's quotation suspended.

Companies of a specialized nature, such as banking and insurance companies, have special statutory requirements, set out either in the Companies Acts or in other Acts. Directors may also incur penalties through the infringement of more general Acts of Parliament, such as the Prevention of Fraud (Investments) Act 1958.

This chapter sets out the major disclosure requirements of the Companies Acts and the stock exchange and other matters that may affect the directors. The detailed requirements of the statements of standard accounting practice (SSAPs) issued by the Accounting Standards Committee will be dealt with in the next chapter.

In addition to the requirements set out, the directors have an overriding responsibility to make sure that they have sufficient information available to enable them to manage the company's affairs effectively and to safeguard its assets. Good accounting practice may also indicate disclosures that should be made, whether or not these are incorporated into SSAPs. Where items require disclosure in the accounts or in the directors' report it is not appropriate to include them in the Chairman's Statement. Wherever disclosure is required the corresponding value for the previous year must be shown.

The director's position

Clarity as to the role of the director is necessary if the underlying implications of some of his decisions are to be apparent. What is his function and to whom is he accountable? Many points of view are advanced and certain of his responsibilities are defined by statute.

Non-statutory responsibilities

The director's role has been variously defined as trustee, agent, manager, etc. One acceptable definition is that directors are 'agents having a fiduciary relationship to their principal, the company'. Does this go far enough and do their responsibilities extend beyond the company to its owners—the shareholders? A point of view which expresses that relationship more effectively is that 'they are stewards managing the business on behalf of its owners, the shareholders'.

The directors may also act as managers in the day-to-day running of the business. This aspect of their work does not differ materially from that of any other manager and it is their responsibilities as directors with which we are concerned in this chapter.

Statutory and other requirements

There are specific statutory requirements, such as those relating to the keeping of proper books of account. There are, however, more general requirements arising from the director's fiduciary relationship with the company. These can be expressed in terms of the recommendations of the Jenkins Committee: 'A director of a company should observe the utmost good faith towards the company in any transaction with it or on its behalf and should act honestly in the exercise of his powers and the discharge of the duties of his office.'

In a memorandum to the President of the Board of Trade in 1969 the Institute of Chartered Accountants recommended that future legislation should make these requirements more explicit in the following form:

1. A director should observe the utmost good faith towards the company in any transaction with it or on its behalf, and should act honestly in the best interests of the company in exercising his powers and discharging the duties of his office, and in connection therewith should exercise the degree of care, diligence and skill that a reasonable prudent director or officer would exercise in comparable circumstances.
2. A director of a company should not make use of any money or other property of the company or of any information acquired by virtue of his position of director or officer of the company to gain directly or indirectly an improper advantage for himself or any other person.
3. A director who commits a breach of these provisions should be liable to the company for any profit made by him and for any damage suffered by the company as a result of the breach.

4. These provisions should be in addition to and not in derogation of any other provisions in companies legislation or any other enactments or rule of law relating to the duties and liabilities of directors of a company.

In addition to the strictly statutory requirements, directors are also concerned with the demands of government departments and bodies, such as the stock exchange, and subject to codes of practice such as the code for take-overs and mergers. Such requirements may not have legal force and if there is any conflict with the best interests of the company competent professional advice should be sought.

Books of account and records

The Companies Act 1948 (CA 1948) s 147 requires directors to ensure that:
1. Proper books of account are maintained to record:
   (a) all receipts and payments;
   (b) all sales and purchases;
   (c) all assets and liabilities.
2. Such books must provide sufficient detail to give a true and fair view of the state of the company's affairs and to explain its transactions.

Where a company is wound up, the above requirements are amplified by CA 1948 s 331, which states that proper books of account should be such that:
1. They explain the transactions and the financial position.
2. They contain day-to-day entries for all cash received and paid.
3. They include where appropriate:
   (a) annual stock sheets;
   (b) records of goods sold and purchased, with sufficient detail to enable the goods and purchasers and sellers to be identified, except in the case of sales in the retail trade.

Penalties can be imposed if such records have not been kept throughout the two years prior to winding up, unless the director can show that he acted honestly and in the circumstances the default was excusable.

In practice, the above requirements necessitate detailed records of:
1. Cash—of all cheques and cash received and paid, suitably identified.
2. Debtors or accounts receivable, and creditors or accounts payable, in sufficient detail to enable amounts owing to individual suppliers or owing by individual customers to be identified and related to supporting documents.
3. Expenditure on long-term assets.
4. Stocks and work in progress. In most cases this will require detailed stock records by item and individual work in progress records.

General requirement as to accounts

The following are the general requirements for the presentation of accounts to the shareholders:

1. A balance sheet and profit and loss account must be laid before the company at least once a year (CA 1948 s 148(1)).
2. Every balance sheet and profit and loss account must show a true and fair view of the state of affairs at the balance sheet date, and of the profit for the year ended on that date (CA 1948 s 149(1) and 152(1)).
3. The statutory requirements as to form and content of the accounts must be adhered to (CA 1948 s 149(2) and (3) and s 152(3)).
4. Where the company has one or more subsidiary companies, group accounts must also be presented (CA 1948 s 150).
5. The accounts must be signed by two directors (or the sole director) after approval by the board (CA 1948 s 155 and 156).

The balance sheet

The full disclosure requirements for the balance sheet and the profit and loss account (dealt with in the following section) are set out in the second Schedule CA 1967. Note that no particular layout is prescribed, merely matters that must be included.

The major disclosure requirements are:
1. Main groupings: the authorized and issued share capital, reserves, provisions, liabilities and assets should be summarized under headings appropriate to the company's business.
2. Fixed assets: these must be stated at cost or valuation less any provision for depreciation and the methods used to arrive at the book value disclosed. The value of assets acquired or disposed of during the year must be shown separately.
3. Investments: investments in unquoted shares of other companies pose valuation problems. The directors are required either to place an estimated value on the shares or to provide the following information relating to them:
    (a) How much of the company's income is derived from the investment?
    (b) What is the company's share of both pre- and post-tax profits of the companies invested in and of their accumulated profits?
    (c) How have such companies' losses been dealt with?
4. Reserves and provisions (other than provisions for depreciation or diminution in value): the reasons for changes in the amount shown as compared with the previous year should be separately disclosed.
5. Loans (other than bank loans or overdrafts): the amount of loans repayable more than five years after the balance sheet date must be disclosed separately. If security has been given by charging some of the company's assets the fact must be stated.
6. Deferred taxation: any amount set aside for the purpose of preventing undue fluctuations in charges for taxation must be stated. (See chapter 3, page 27.)

7. Contingent liabilities: the nature of any contingent liabilities and, if practical, the estimated amount.
8. Future capital expenditure: the estimated amount divided between expenditure contracted for and that authorized but not contracted for.
9. Current assets: these must be stated at a value not greater than they would realize in the ordinary course of business. This would require provisions to be made for possible bad debts and for defective, obsolete and slow-moving stocks. The basis on which the value of stocks and work in progress has been arrived at must be stated.

The profit and loss account

Major items which require disclosure in the profit and loss account are:
1. Turnover: the amount of turnover for the period.
2. Depreciation: the amount charged against the year's profit in respect of depreciation.
3. Interest: this must be divided into interest payable on bank loans, overdrafts, and other loans repayable more than five years after the balance sheet date and interest on other loans.
4. Tax: the basis and composition of the charge for UK and overseas taxation.
5. Income from investments: income receivable from quoted investments, unquoted investments, and rents from land should be separately distinguished.
6. Reserves: any amounts transferred to or from reserves.
7. Hire of equipment: the cost of hiring plant and equipment.
8. Dividends: the aggregate of dividends paid or proposed.
9. Items relating to the previous year(s): any income or expenditure which relates to prior years must be disclosed separately from the results for the current year.
10. Exceptional transactions: if the profit is materially affected by a transaction of a kind not usually undertaken by the company or by circumstances of an exceptional or non-recurring nature, or by a change in the basis of accounting, the effect should be disclosed separately from the results for the year.
11. Directors' remuneration: details of the directors' and the chairman's remuneration must be shown.

Where any items are not shown in the body of the accounts they must be shown by way of a note to the accounts.

The directors' report

A directors' report must be attached to every balance sheet laid before the company in general meeting (CA 1948 s 157(1)). Prior to the 1967 Companies Act the directors' report carried little of interest. That Act, however, set out a number of matters which must be included in the report and it now forms an important part of the annual report to shareholders. Matters which require disclosure are listed below.

1. Directors:
   (a) the names of persons who at any time during the year acted as directors (CA 1967 s 16(1));
   (b) any material interest in contracts with the company (other than a contract of service), including arrangements for the directors to acquire shares in or debentures of the company or any other body corporate (CA 1967 s 16);
   (c) interests of the directors in shares or debentures of the company (CA 1967 s 16).
2. Activities:
   (a) The principal activities of the company and its subsidiaries and any changes therein;
   (b) the proportion of turnover and profits attributable to classes of business which differ materially from each other (CA 1967 s 17).
3. Fixed assets:
   (a) if any significant changes took place in fixed assets, particulars of such changes (CA 1967 s 16);
   (b) if an interest in land is held by the company and its market value differs substantially from the balance sheet value, the difference must be stated with as sufficient degree of precision as is possible.
4. Issues of shares or debentures: where the company has issued shares or debentures during the year the reason for the issue, the number of shares or amount of debentures issued, and the consideration received (CA 1967 s 16).
5. Employees: unless the number of employees is less than 100, the number of employees on average in each week of the year and the aggregate remuneration (CA 1967 s 18).
6. Donations: amounts given by the company for charitable or political purposes and, in the case of political donations, the names of the recipients and the amount received (CA 1967 s 19).
7. Exports: unless the total turnover is less than £100 000, the value of goods exported or a statement that no exports have been made (CA 1967 s 20).
8. Dividends and reserves: the recommended dividend and amounts to be transferred to reserves (CA 1948 s 157).
9. State of affairs: any matters other than those dealt with above, which are material for the appreciation of the state of the company's affairs by its members must be disclosed unless to do so would be harmful to the business of the company. This would include any events occurring after the balance sheet date and therefore properly excluded from the accounts, of which the directors are aware when preparing the report.

Delegation and limitation of responsibility

If the company is in default of any of the provisions outlined, it will be a defence for the director to prove that he had reasonable grounds for believing and did in fact so believe that a competent and reliable person was charged with the duty of seeing that the provisions of the Companies Acts were observed and that person was in a position to discharge that duty (CA 1948 s 148, 149, 150). In making such a delegation the directors must act honestly and diligently and with reasonable skill and care.

While the responsibilities of directors are collective, each director may have a special area of responsibility within the company. The director then has a special duty in relation to that sector and is expected to be aware of all material factors arising from that section's operations which affect the accounts of the company and should ensure that the other directors are fully informed where any such facts would affect the true and fair view as shown by the accounts.

Stock exchange

Where application is made for the shares of a company to be quoted on the stock exchange the directors are required to give an undertaking to provide information additional to that required under the Companies Acts. This additional information includes:

—A statement of persons holding or beneficially interested in any substantial part of the company's share capital and the amount involved.

—Interim profit figures, i.e., profit for the first six months of the year.

—Whether or not the company is a close company. (See chapter 4, p. 40.)

—A geographical analysis of turnover and profit.

EEC

The EEC is in the process of issuing a number of directives relating to companies. As these become final they will become a part of UK law and apply to UK companies. The first of these is already in operation and requires, for example, the company number and country of registration to be included in letter heads, etc.

It is likely that ultimately a community company law will be established which provides for the formation of a European company able to operate across the whole EEC.

SSAPs

Statements of standard accounting practice have already been issued covering the areas listed below.

SSAP 1. Accounting for the results of associated companies.

SSAP 2. Disclosure of accounting policies.

SSAP 3. Earnings per share.

SSAP 4.   Accounting treatment of government grants.
SSAP 5.   Accounting for value added tax.
SSAP 6.   Extraordinary items and prior year adjustments.
SSAP 7.   Accounting for changes in the purchasing power of money (provisional standard only).
SSAP 8.   Treatment of taxation under the imputation system in the accounts of companies.
SSAP 9.   Stocks and work in progress.
SSAP 10. Statements of sources and applications of funds.
SSAP 11. Accounting for deferred taxation.

A series of International Accounting Standards are also being published. Should these conflict with SSAPs the latter will prevail, and they will not, therefore, be considered further.

Prospectuses and similar statements

The directors of a company are the persons primarily responsible for both the issue and contents of a prospectus. They are bound to state everything with strict accuracy and to omit nothing that could affect a potential investor's judgement on the issue.

When making an issue of share capital, or borrowing money, or being involved in a take-over bid, the board will usually be working closely with professional advisers and institutions. Because of the potential civil and criminal liabilities which can fall on the directors, competent advice should be taken in all cases.

3.
Accounting policies and practice

In the preparation and presentation of accounts certain basic rules are applied so that the reader can better understand them and be able to place more reliance on them. Some of the more basic accounting concepts are not written down in an authoritative text but are to be found in the textbooks and general guidelines laid down by the professional bodies for their members. Others relating to more specific matters are included in SSAPs.

Since directors are responsible for the accounts presented to shareholders, they should be aware of the basic concepts governing their presentation and of matters covered by SSAPs and the implications that these may have for the presentation of their own company's accounts. If for any reason it is felt by the board that the company should depart from these rules, then the accounts should make quite explicit the manner and extent to which it has done so, in order that the users of the accounts can interpret them accordingly.

Basic concepts

Business entity

The accounts are a representation of the state of affairs of the business and not of the person or persons who own it. Private transactions of the owners or directors must be kept quite separate from the recording and presentation of the affairs of the business. In the case of large, quoted companies this distinction is seen quite clearly. However, where all the shares of a company are owned by one person or a small group of people this distinction may not be seen so clearly. The directors/owners may see no real difference between their private affairs and the affairs of the company that they own, and as a consequence private transactions may be put through the company's books. If this is the case then any such items must be excluded from the presentation of the company's results and charged to or credited to the director or owner concerned.

Going concern

The basis of valuation of the company's assets included in its balance sheet assumes that the company is to continue in business in the future. Thus fixed assets are valued on the basis of cost or revaluation less the provision for depreciation, and not the amount for which the assets could be sold; stocks of materials and work in progress on the basis that the manufacturing process will be completed and that they, together with stocks of already completed goods, will be sold in the normal course of business. This contrasts with the situation that would prevail if the company is unlikely to continue in business. In such a situation the assets would have to be valued on the basis of what they would fetch on the liquidation of the company. The auditors will give consideration as to whether the going concern basis is appropriate, e.g., in the last accounts published by British Leyland before the government took a majority interest, the auditors noted that the accounts were prepared on a going concern basis only on the assumption that sufficient government support would be forthcoming to keep the company in being. If that support had not been forthcoming then, because of the inability of the company to remain in business, the assets would more properly have been based upon what they would realize on a forced sale.

Conservatism or prudence

The point of this concept is that profits are not to be taken into the accounts until they are realized, but that losses are to be taken in as soon as they can be recognized. A practical application of this concept is the rule that stocks and work in progress are valued at the *lower* of cost or marketable or realizable value.

Sometimes this concept is breached for quite specific reasons. In the case of long-term contracts undertaken by a company in the construction industry, the SSAP dealing with the valuation of stocks and work in progress provides that the profit on such a contract can be taken up year by year during its life, subject to suitable provisions against contingencies, etc. Inflation distorts the unit of measure used to record transactions and this must be compensated for in some way. If not, balance sheet values become less and less representative of the business. Directors may therefore decide to revalue the assets to their present-day values, thus bringing into the accounts a gain in value as measured in monetary units.

Consistency

Having decided upon the accounting policies to be adopted by the company, the directors then have a duty to ensure that those policies are applied consistently year by year. Obviously the reported profit would not be representative of the year's earnings if accounting policies, such as the rate of depreciation and the treatment of research and development costs, were varied at each year end. This does not mean to say that directors cannot vary the accounting policies that they have adopted. They can, but where there is such a change the year's profit must first be computed on the basis that the revised policy had been in effect at *both* the beginning and the end of the year to give a more accurate measure of the year's earnings, and the increase or decrease in earnings due to the change is then reported separately.

Materiality

Directors should see the rule of materiality as providing for the exclusion from separate disclosure in the accounts of numerous non-material items which would tend to obscure the more significant ones. Such a proliferation of items would turn attention away from those factors which matter and interfere with the process of comparison and contrast in analysing the accounts. The rule of materiality can therefore make a positive contribution to clarity in presentation.

What is 'material' when considering the various disclosure provisions in the Companies Acts or other requirements? One cannot define in value terms what is material. A value which is insignificant for a very large company might be crucial for a small one. The judgement of directors and accountants must therefore be qualitative rather than quantitiative. Material in this context can therefore be defined as limiting information that may be required to those matters which an average prudent investor ought reasonably to be acquainted with before purchasing any of the securities of the company. A material fact is one which is likely to influence judgement given the nature of the business and its criteria of performance and is based upon an informed sense of proportion.

SSAP 1. Accounting for the results of associated companies

In considering this SSAP, directors should bear in mind the difference between the company's own accounts and the consolidated group accounts which are also presented when the company has one or more subsidiary companies.

As was seen in chapter 1, where a company has one or more subsidiary companies the company prepares in addition to its own accounts a consolidated balance sheet and profit and loss account, thus providing shareholders with a view of the group as an entity. The requirement to include companies in the consolidated accounts does not apply to those companies where the investing company or group has a 50 per cent or less interest. In the past, the results of those companies which are not subsidiaries but where the investing company has a major interest have been included in its accounts only to the extent of dividends received.

Two important developments in recent years have, however, lead to a revision of that procedure.

1. The practice of conducting parts of the company's business through other companies, whether they are subsidiary companies or not, is growing.

2. Increasing importance is being attached by investors to the measure of earnings.

As a result, it is now deemed necessary for the financial report to include the appropriate share of the profits and losses of 'associated companies' rather than merely the dividends received from such companies.

What is an associated company?

'Associated company' means any company, other than a subsidiary company, where the investing company's or group's interest in the company:
1. Is effectively that of a partner in a joint venture or consortium.
OR
2. Is long term and comprises 20 per cent or more of the equity voting rights and the investing company or group is in a position to exercise a significant influence over the associated company.

An essential ingredient of associated company status in either case is that the investing company or group participates in its commercial and financial policy decisions.

Requirements of the SSAP

1. Profits and losses: where the investing company has no subsidiary companies it should bring into its own profit and loss account its share of the profits and losses and related taxation of all material associated companies. Where the investing company has subsidiaries (and therefore presents consolidated accounts) it will bring into its own accounts only the dividends received or receivable from associated companies for the period. However, the group's share of the profits, etc., of associated companies will be brought into the consolidated accounts.

   In both cases the amount attributable to associated companies should be separately shown and suitably described. The investing group's share of the aggregate profits less losses retained in associated companies should be shown separately.
2. Balance sheet: the value of the investing company or group's interest in associated companies should be shown at:
   (a) valuation,
   OR
   (b) the cost of the investment less any amounts written off plus the investing group's share of post-acquisition retained profits and reserves.
3. Particulars of associated companies: the names of and interests in each associated company should be shown, and also the same details for any other company in which 20 per cent or more of the equity voting rights are held but which is not treated as an associated company.

SSAP 2. Disclosure of accounting policies

The diversity of business enterprises is such that it is not possible to lay down the specific accounting bases of valuation that should be followed by each company. The directors must use their judgement as to which accounting bases are the most appropriate for the type of business that their company undertakes and adopt these as a matter of policy in the preparation of their accounts.

Since different accounting bases may be quite properly used by different companies, it is fundamental to the understanding and interpretation of accounts that those who use them should be aware of what accounting policies are being followed. This statement therefore requires that the accounting policies laid down by the board for dealing with material items should be disclosed by way of a note to the accounts.

Material factors for which different accounting bases are recognized and for which a policy must be decided include:

—Depreciation of fixed assets.
—The treatment and amortization of such items as research and development expenditure, patents and trade marks.
—Stocks and work in progress.
—Long-term contracts.
—Deferred taxation.
—Hire purchase and instalment transactions.
—Leasing and rental transactions.
—Conversion of foreign currencies.
—Repairs and renewals.
—Consolidation policies.
—Property development transactions.
—Warranties for products and services.

SSAP 3. Earnings per share

Since the UK changed to corporation tax as the method of taxing companies, earnings have become an important element in an investor's decision to invest. The usual measure used for this purpose is the price/earnings ratio (P/E), that is to say, the earnings attributable to each ordinary share divided into the current market price of the share—e.g., if the earnings per share is 5p and the current share price is 50p then the shares are being traded on a P/E of 10. Since investors are looking at a range of possible investments for the purpose of identifying investment opportunities, it is desirable that the earnings per share element in the P/E ratio should be calculated and disclosed on a comparable basis.

The statement is applicable to all quoted companies and requires that the EPS be disclosed on the 'net' basis, and, if materially different, on the 'nil' distribution basis.

Net basis Profit before tax and before extraordinary items
    less taxation
    less minority interests
    less preference dividends
    equals profit attributable to equity shareholders

$$\text{EPS} = \frac{\text{profit attributable to equity shareholders}}{\text{number of shares issued ranking for dividends}}$$

The deduction of taxation above includes any irrecoverable Advance Corporation Tax (ACT) and unrelieved overseas tax. (See chapter 4.)

'Nil' basis This is calculated on the same basis used for the 'net' basis with the exception that the tax deduction excludes irrecoverable ACT and unrelieved overseas tax except so far as they apply to preference dividends.

Where the company has issued shares which do not rank for dividend but which may do so at some future time, or has issued securities which are convertible into ordinary shares, the fully diluted EPS must also be disclosed if the dilution is material, in this case 5 per cent or more.

SSAP 4. The accounting treatment of government grants

The purpose of this standard is to secure a common accounting treatment of capital based grants under the Industry Act 1972 and similar acts elsewhere. Two methods may be used, both of which are designed to credit the grant to revenue over the expected useful life of the asset.

1. Reduce the cost of the asset acquired by the amount of the grant, thus reducing future depreciation expense.
2. Treat the grant as a deferred credit, a part of which will be transferred to revenue each year. Such deferred credits should be shown separately, in the balance sheet and not as part of the shareholders' funds.

SSAP 5. Accounting for value added tax

VAT is designed to be borne by the ultimate consumer and is not normally a charge on the business enterprise. The turnover shown in the profit and loss account should exclude VAT on taxable outputs. If for some reason it is felt desirable to show the gross turnover, the VAT should be deducted so as to show the turnover net of tax. Any irrecoverable VAT allocated to fixed assets should be included in their cost if practical and material.

SSAP 6. Extraordinary and prior year adjustments

Prior to this statement, extraordinary and prior year adjustments were dealt with in one of two ways:

1. To include in the profit and loss account only the recurring activities of

the business and to take extraordinary and prior year items direct to
reserves.
2. To state separately in the profit and loss account all extraordinary items
recognized in that year and with certain exceptions all prior year items.
The statement is based upon the adoption of the second procedure above as
standard practice.

What are extraordinary items?

Extraordinary items are those items related to transactions outside the
ordinary activities of the business which are both material and not expected
to recur frequently or regularly.

What are prior year adjustments?

Prior year adjustments are material adjustments relating to earlier years
arising from changes in accounting policies and the correction of fundamental
errors. They do not include normal correcting adjustments of accounting
estimates made in earlier years.

Disclosure in the profit and loss account

Extraordinary items less any attributable taxation should be shown separately
in the profit and loss account for the year and appear after the results for that
year's ordinary activities (less taxation) have been shown. Also the nature
and size of the extraordinary items should be disclosed.

Prior year adjustments should be dealt with by restating the values for the
earlier years which will result in the opening balance of retained profit being
suitably adjusted. The effect of the change should be disclosed where practical
by showing separately in the restatement of the previous year's figures the
amount involved.

SSAP 7. Accounting for changes in the purchasing power of money

This SSAP is dealt with in chapter 14.

SSAP 8. The treatment of taxation under the imputation system in the accounts of companies

This statement deals with the implications of the imputation system of
corporation tax dealt with in chapter 4 in so far as they present problems
in the presentation of the financial report.

Treatment of outgoing dividends and the related advanced corporation tax (ACT)

The charge for corporation tax (CT) in the profit and loss account should
represent the full corporation tax liability on those profits and not be reduced
by the ACT that can be offset against that liability. The amount shown as the

cost of the dividends for the period will therefore be the actual amount declared and will not include the related tax credit.

Recoverability of ACT

ACT is recoverable against the CT liability for the year in which the dividend is paid. If the profits for that year are insufficient for ACT to be recovered, the unabsorbed ACT can be set off against the corporation tax payable for the two previous years. Any ACT then unrelieved can be carried forward indefinitely.

At the time of presenting the accounts it is necessary to decide whether the recovery of ACT is reasonably certain or whether it should be written off in that year's profit and loss account, although it might be possible to recover it at some time in the future. Unless it is reasonably certain that it can be recovered in the next accounting period or can be offset in the future against deferred taxation of profits it should be written off. If material, the amount of irrecoverable ACT should be stated separately in the tax charge shown in the profit and loss account.

Unrelieved overseas tax

If overseas tax becomes unrelievable through the payment of a dividend in excess of UK earnings, the amount, if material, should be separately specified in the tax charge.

Incoming dividends from UK resident companies

Incoming dividends should be included at an amount representing the amount of the dividend plus the tax credit. The equivalent of the tax credit is then included in the tax charged in the accounts.

Balance sheet

The amount of the proposed dividend should be included in current liabilities. The related ACT should be included as a current tax liability and if the ACT is recoverable either an equivalent amount deducted from any deferred tax account or shown as a deferred asset. If it is irrecoverable it should be added to the year's tax charge as discussed earlier.

Where the rate of corporation tax for the year is not known (it is fixed in the budget at the end of the fiscal year) the latest known rate should be used in the accounts.

SSAP 9. Stocks and work in progress

This statement deals with the valuation of stocks and work in progress and its presentation in the financial statement. The question of valuation is related to two types of stocks and work in progress—that related to long-term contracts and that related to other types of stocks.

Stocks and work in progress other than long-term contract work in progress

The application of the matching concept requires that all costs are matched with the related revenues. The stocks and work in progress on hand at the end of a period must be valued on the basis of the expenditure incurred upon them in the normal course of business (which would include all related production overheads) if this is to be achieved.

Each item of stock should be dealt with individually in the valuation process except in such cases as retailing, where the company owns a large number of rapidly changing individual items. In such a case valuation may be made on selling price less a deduction for the normal gross margin.

The value at which stocks and work in progress are stated should be the total of the lower of cost or net realizable value of each item of stock and work in progress or groups of similar items. (Net realizable value is the amount that could be realized if the item was to be sold, less the costs of disposal.)

Long-term contract work in progress

If the profit from such contracts is only taken when the contract is complete the annual profit will reflect the profit on contracts completed and not the value of the work done during the period. To present a fairer view of the profits for the period the profits attributable to the work done during the period should be included in that period's profit and in the value of the work in progress—less, of course, any necessary provision for contingencies. Directors must, however, consider whether, given the nature of the contracts, it is reasonable to foresee profits in advance of the completion of the contracts.

Disclosure in the financial statement

The accounting policies used in calculating cost, net realizable value, attributable profit, and foreseeable losses where appropriate, should be stated. Stocks and work in progress should be sub-classified in the balance sheet or in notes to the financial statement in a manner appropriate to the business and so as to indicate the amounts held in each of the main categories.

In respect of long-term contracts there should be stated:
1. The amount of work in progress at cost plus attributable profit, less foreseeable losses.
2. Cash received and receivable at the balance sheet date as progress payments on account of contracts in progress.

SSAP 10. Statements of sources and applications of funds

The purpose of this statement is to ensure that shareholders are presented with a statement of the sources from which the company has derived its funds and how they have been used within the company. It applies to all companies with sales or gross income in excess of £25 000 per annum. This statement is derived principally from a comparison of the balance sheet at the beginning of the year with that at the end of the year. The minimum disclosure required includes:

—The profit or loss of the period.

—Adjustments for items which do not involve a funds flow, e.g., depreciation.

—Dividends paid.

—Acquisitions and disposals of fixed and other non-current assets.

—Funds movements due to changes in long-term borrowing or issued capital.

—Increases and decreases in working capital subdivided into its component parts, and movements in net liquid funds.

SSAP 11. Accounting for deferred taxation

There can be considerable differences between the amount of profits on which the taxation for the period is based and the reported profit for the year as shown in the financial statements. For example, in computing the profits on which tax has to be paid the company might deduct 100 per cent of the cost of fixed assets as a capital allowance, but only take up the relevant amount of depreciation in its financial statement. It is felt that it is wrong that one period should benefit from such timing differences and others suffer. The basis of the statement therefore is that the reported profits for each period should have deducted from them a provision for taxation based upon the rate of tax on the reported profits. The difference between that amount of tax and the tax actually paid should then be taken into a deferred tax account and gradually released as the timing differences are reversed.

Timing differences

Timing differences can arise from:

1. Accelerated capital allowances, e.g., 100 per cent first year allowances.
2. Expenses for which provision has been made in the accounts but which are not allowable for tax until a later period.
3. Income taken into the accounts but which is not taxable until a later period.

Methods of computing the deferred tax account

The deferred tax accounts may be based upon one of two methods.

The deferral method The amounts of tax taken into the deferred tax account represent the timing differences at the then tax rate. If the tax rates change subsequently, no change is made in the provision of deferred tax.

The liability method This assumes that the timing differences are liabilities that the company will have to meet at some future time. When, therefore, the rate of tax changes the unreversed timing differences are adjusted to the new rate of tax.

Revaluation of assets

Where the value of assets is written up in the accounts this would give a possible charge to tax, if the asset was to be sold at the revalued figure, under the following headings:

1. Capital gains tax.
2. A balancing charge or restriction on the value of future capital allowances.

The surplus arising on revaluation should be divided into two elements: the tax that would be levied if the asset was to be sold at the new value, and the increase in value less the amount of tax so calculated. The former amount is taken to the deferred tax account, the latter to reserves.

Disclosure in the financial statements

The method adopted, i.e., the deferral method or the liability method, should be disclosed as an accounting policy.

Profit and loss account The taxation effect of timing differences should be disclosed separately as a component of the total tax charge, or by way of note. If they relate to extraordinary items they should be shown separately as a part of such items. Any subsequent adjustments to take into account changes in the rate of tax under the liability method should be separately disclosed.

Balance sheet The balance of the deferred tax account should be shown separately in the balance sheet and described as deferred taxation. It should not be shown as a part of shareholders' funds nor included in current assets or liabilities. A note to the accounts should indicate the nature and amount of the major elements included. Where deferred taxation arises from movements in reserves, e.g., from revaluation of an asset, the amounts transferred to or from the deferred taxation account should be shown separately as part of such movements.

4.
Taxation

Note: References are to the Income and Corporation Taxes Act 1970.

Directors cannot be expected to have a detailed knowledge of tax law, unless this happens to be their particular specialism. They should, however, have a sufficient knowledge of the general framework of the tax system to enable them to recognize that many of their decisions have tax consequences. In their decision-making processes the directors should ensure that these tax consequences are fully considered before the decision is made, rather than making the decision and at a later date having to hand over the problem of sorting out the tax consequences to a specialist. It may then be too late to minimize the tax burden. This is particularly true when a decision is made to set up an overseas business operation where consideration must be given to the legal form the operation should take, i.e., subsidiary company, branch, etc., and whether the interest should be held through the intermediary of other countries. Overseas taxation and the double tax agreements entered into between different countries are too complex to deal with in a book of this nature and professional advice should be sought at a very early stage in the consideration of such proposals.

This chapter confines itself to the basic framework of taxation for both individuals and companies, including capital gains tax (CGT) and capital transfer tax (CTT).

Who and what is taxable?

Broadly speaking, all persons who are resident in the UK are subject to UK taxation on the whole of their income world-wide. What is construed as as residence is a matter of fact which is determined by such criteria as length of stay in the country, frequency of visits, and maintenance of a residence in this country. In any situation where a person is likely to spend a substantial part of his time overseas, or invests in or sets up a business overseas, specialist advice should be sought. Corporations are normally resident in the country from which the *control* of the business is exercised irrespective of the country of registration, that is to say the country in which board meetings are held and executive decisions taken. Persons who are resident overseas are subject to UK tax on that part of their income which arises in the UK.

The strict application of the above rules, and similar rules in force in overseas countries would mean that income could be taxed twice—once in the overseas country and again in the UK. To avoid the worst effects that would arise from this situation, double taxation agreements are in force with most foreign countries which provide for double tax relief. Some of the double tax agreements provide that certain classes of income are taxable in only one of the countries which are parties to the agreement. In other cases the income is taxable in each of the countries but the tax paid overseas is used to reduce the UK tax payable. In other words, the taxpayer effectively pays tax at the highest of the UK or the overseas rate.

Where no double tax agreement is in force then unilateral relief may be available which allows the tax suffered overseas to be set off against the UK tax liability, or if this is not allowed, then the overseas tax can be deducted from the foreign income in computing the amount that is taxable in the UK.

Income tax

By whom payable?

Income tax is payable by individuals and parternships.

What is income?

Lord Macnaghten in *London County Council v. A-G* stated 'Income tax, if I may be pardoned for saying so, is a tax on income. It is not meant to be a tax on anything else'. On this basis casual profits, e.g., from selling a picture one has had for many years (where one is not a dealer in pictures) are excluded from the charge to tax. This is, however, somewhat circumscribed by the Norman Wisdom case where the actor had invested money in silver bullion and made a profit on its realization. The gain was held to be subject to income tax. (This was before the introduction of capital gains tax. If it had been held to be free of income tax it would today, in any case, be subject to capital gains tax.)

To be taxable, the income should arise from one of the sources outlined in the five schedules set out in Table 4.1. The bases of assessment of each of the schedules varies and the Table shows the basis of assessment of each.

Schedule D, Cases I and II

For those who engage in business or a profession, the rules relating to these two cases are the most important. They also have some relevance to companies, since the timing of corporation tax payments may be determined by the timing of that company's income tax payments when it was subject to

TABLE 4.1
The schedules and the bases of assessment

Schedule	Income assessable	Basis of assessment
A	Income from land and buildings (from 1970/71)	Actual income of the year
B	Woodlands (except where an election is made for assessment under Sch. D)	⅓ of the annual value of the land
C	Profits payable out of the public revenue through a UK agent	Assessed on the agent who pays the income to the recipient net of tax
D Case I	Profits of trades or businesses	Normally the preceding year basis
D Case II	Income from professions and vocations	
D Case III	Interest not taxed at source	
D Case IV	Income from foreign securities	As above, but see note 3
D Case V	Income from foreign possessions	
D Case VI	Any other annual profits or gains	
E	Emoluments from any office or employment where recipient is:	Actual income arising
E Case I	Resident in the UK	Full amount arising but see notes 1 and 2 below
E Case II	Non-resident, or if resident not ordinarily resident in the UK	
E Case III	Resident in the UK	Any amounts not assessed under Cases I and II and remitted to the UK in that year or any other year in which he was resident.

Note 1. Where the employment is carried out wholly outside the UK and is unrelated to any employment in the UK then:
    1. If the person is absent from the UK for a continuous period of 365 days or more (visits to the UK not exceeding 63 consecutive days or a total of one-sixth of the period of absence does not interrupt the continuous period) a deduction of 100 per cent of the income can be made from the overseas income.
    2. Where the continuous period of absence is less than 365 days 25 per cent can be deducted from the overseas income.
Note 2. Where the emoluments are 'foreign emoluments', that is to say, the earnings of a person not domiciled in the UK from an employment with an employer not resident in the UK, a deduction of 50 per cent from the earnings may be allowed. If the duties are performed wholly outside the UK the earnings are exempt from UK tax.
Note 3. Foreign pensions or annuities are assessed on 90 per cent of the amount arising in the preceding year, whether remitted or not, but if the person is not domiciled in the UK or not ordinarily resident the amounts remitted only. Income from trades is assessed on 75 per cent of the income arising.

income tax. The 'preceding year' basis for tax assessment means that in normal cases the basis for the tax assessment in any tax year is the profits for the accounting period ended in the previous tax year. Thus if the business year ends on 31 December each year, then for the tax year 1976/77 the amount of the assessment is based upon the profits for the accounting period ended on 31 December 1975.

In the early years it is not possible to use this basis since there is no accounting period ended in the previous tax year and special rules apply. Similarly there are special rules for the closing years of a business.

Early years

In the early years the basis of assessment is as follows:
1. Years in which the business commences: the actual profits earned in the tax year.
2. The second tax year: the profits for the first year's trading (except where the first accounting period ended on 5 April, in which case the normal rules can apply).
3. The third tax year: the normal rules apply.

Take the case of a person who starts a business on 1 July 1976 so that the accounts for the first year's trading are made up to 30 June 1977. These accounts show a profit of £1200. The assessments to tax for the first three tax years would be as follows:

Tax year 1976/7: 9/12 of £1200　　= 　£900
Tax year 1977/8: first year's profit = £1200
Tax year 1978/9: normal basis 　　 = £1200

It can be seen from the above that the first year's trading will in almost all cases determine the first three years' tax assessments.

Section 117 claim

Where the actual profits earned in the second and third tax years are lower than the amounts that would be assessed under the above rules, the tax payer has the option to have the assessment for *both* years based on the actual profits earned in each of the tax years.

Let us assume that the business used in the above example earned profits in its next two years' trading as follows:

Trading year to 30 June 1978 = 　£800
Trading year to 30 June 1979 = £1300

The taxpayer could elect to have the assessments amended to:

Tax year 1977/8: $\frac{1}{4}$ of £1200 plus
$\frac{3}{4}$of £800 　　 = 　£900
Tax year 1978/9: $\frac{1}{4}$ of £800 plus
$\frac{3}{4}$ of £1300 　 = £1175

The election must be made for both of the tax years, not just for one of them.

Closing years

The assessments for the final, penultimate and pre-penultimate years can be adjusted to the actual profit for each of the years at the option of the Inland Revenue.

Losses from trading

Losses arising from trading can be relieved in the following ways:
1. Section 168: by set-off against other income for the year.
2. Section 171: by carry forward and set-off against future profits *from the same trade.*
3. Terminal losses can be carried back and set off against the profits of the three preceding years.

Payment of tax

The payment of the tax due in any fiscal year is made in two instalments as far as earned income is concerned. One payment is made on the 1 January in the fiscal year and the second instalment on the following 1 July. Tax on other income is paid in one payment on 1 January.

Basic and higher band rates of tax

Where the total income less personal and other allowances is less than £5000, tax is payable at the basic rate of 35 per cent (1976/7). Income above this level is divided into bands and successive bands are taxed at higher rates until, when the £20 000 level is reached, the rate of tax on additional income is 83 per cent.

Investment income surcharge

Dividends from companies are received together with the related tax credit and there is therefore no further basic tax to pay. There may, however, be tax due at higher band rates, and, in addition, if the total investment income exceeds £1000 the income is subject to a 10 per cent investment income surcharge on the excess, and if the investment income exceeds £2000 the surcharge is at the rate of 15 per cent.

Husband and wife

The income of a wife is deemed for tax purposes to be that of the husband and he is liable for the payment of tax on the combined income. This can be modified in two ways.
1. Separate assessment (sections 33 and 39): the assessment is divided between the husband and wife but the total amount of tax payable is not affected.
2. Separate taxation (Finance Act 1971 Section 23 and Schedule 4): if the husband and wife jointly make the required election the wife will then be taxed on *earned* income as though she were a single person. The husband is then taxed on the balance of the joint incomes as though he were a single person. The election must be made not earlier than six months before or later than six months after the year of assessment. It then continues until revoked.

Capital allowances and grants

Capital expenditure and related charges on income, e.g., depreciation, are not allowable expenses for tax purposes. However, relief is given for certain specific classes of capital expenditure under what is now the Capital Allowances Act 1968. The capital allowance system applies to both individuals and companies.

Classes of expenditure for which relief is available

—Industrial buildings and structures (this excludes commercial buildings, e.g., office blocks, warehouses, hotels, except where, for example the office or warehouse forms an integral part of the industrial buildings).
—Machinery and plant.
—Vehicles.
—Mines, oil wells.
—Dredging.
—Agricultural land and buildings.
—Scientific research.
—Patent rights.
—Know-how.
—Ships.
—Cemeteries and crematoria.

Capital allowances

For most types of capital expenditure two allowances are given: *First year allowances* in the year of acquisition (initial allowances in the case of buildings) and, *annual writing down allowances* in subsequent years, or *allowances related to depletion*, e.g., extraction of mineral deposits.

In order to be entitled to the allowances the asset must become the property of the trader some time during the year and be brought into use. The first year allowances can be partially or wholly disclaimed within two years of the accounting period, any amounts disclaimed then fall to be recouped in the form of annual writing down allowances in subsequent years.

Rates of allowance (1975)

	First year allowance	Annual writing down allowance
Industrial buildings	50%	4% straight line on the cost
Agricultural buildings	nil	10% of the cost in each of the first 10 years
Machinery, plant and vehicles (except private motor cars)	100%	25% on the reducing balance

	First year allowance	Annual writing down allowance
Motor cars (the allowances given will not exceed £5000)	nil	25% on the reducing balance (including the year of acquisition)
Scientific research	100%	—
Patent rights and know-how	—	$\frac{1}{17}$ of the cost of buying the patent over 17 years, and $\frac{1}{6}$ of the cost of buying know-how over 6 years
Ships	100%	—

The pool account

From the point of view of recording capital allowances, as from 26 October 1970 all plant, machinery, vehicles, etc., can be included in a single pool account calculation. Assets acquired before that date still require separate calculation of capital allowances and the ability to identify the allowances claimed on individual items of plant and equipment. The pool account contains the cost of assets acquired, receipts from disposals of assets, and the capital allowances taken. The pool account calculation for a year might look like the example below.

	Pool account	*Capital allowances for the year*
	£	£
Written down value brought forward from previous year	4770	
Less: Receipts from disposals during the current year	200	
	4570	
Less: Annual writing down allowances 25% on the balance brought forward less disposals	1143	1143
	3427	
Add: Expenditure on acquisitions for the year 4000		
Less: First year allowance 4000	—	4000

	Pool account	*Capital allowances for the year*
Written down value carried forward to future years	3427	
Capital allowances for the year		5143

Balancing charge

When the pool account shows a negative value after deducting the receipts from disposals it is treated as a negative capital allowance and called a *balancing charge*.

Corporation tax

Who and what is taxable?

Companies resident in the UK — on world income.

Companies not resident in the UK carrying on business through a branch or agency — on profits attributable to agency including capital gains on UK disposals.

Company

'Company' in the context of corporation tax means any body corporate or unincorporated associations, e.g., a cricket club.

Profits

'Profits' in the context of corporation tax mean income plus capital gains, but excluding dividends from UK companies.

Basis of assessment

The assessment for corporation tax is based upon the profits actually earned during the corporation tax year (the corporation tax year begins on 1 April and is denominated by the year in which it commences, i.e., the corporation tax year commencing on 1 April 1978 is the 1978 corporation tax year).

Take as an example a company which has an accounting period for the twelve months ending on 31 December 1977, and the profits for that period are £12 000. Assume the tax rates for the corporation tax years 1976 and 1977 are 50 per cent and 55 per cent respectively. Tax will be paid as follows:

$$
\begin{array}{lll}
\text{Year 1976: } \tfrac{1}{4} \text{ of £12 000 @ 50\%} & = & \text{£1500} \\
\text{Year 1977: } \tfrac{3}{4} \text{ of £12 000 @ 55\%} & = & \text{£4950} \\
\\
\text{Tax payable on the year's profits} & & \text{£6450}
\end{array}
$$

Rate of tax

The rate of corporation tax is announced in the budget at the *end* of the tax year, e.g., the rate for the corporation tax year 1978 is announced in the budget statement in 1979. For illustrative purposes in this section the normal corporation tax rate is taken as being 50 per cent and the basic rate of personal tax at 30 per cent.

Payment of corporation tax

Corporation tax will in most cases be paid in two parts. *Advance corporation tax* (ACT) is tax attributable to dividends and other distributions, while *mainstream corporation tax* is the total corporation tax due less the amount of ACT that can be set off against the corporation tax liability. ACT is payable within 14 days after the end of each 'return period' (normally a calendar quarter).

Mainstream corporation tax is payable nine months after the end of the accounting period, unless the company was in existence on 5 April 1965. In that case the payment of corporation tax is made after the same interval of time as existed under the old income tax rules (companies paid income tax in one payment on 1 January). Thus a company which had an accounting period to 30 June would not have paid the income tax related to a year's earnings until 1 January of the next but one year, e.g., for the year to 30 June 1963 income tax would have been paid on 1 January 1965. This delay in payment of 18 months is preserved under the corporation tax system.

Losses

Losses arising from a trade can be dealt with as follows.

Section 177(2) The loss can be set off against total profits (including capital gains) for the accounting period. It may also be set off against the total profits of the immediately preceding accounting period of equal length.

Section 177(1) The loss can be set off against future profits *of the same trade* and surplus franked investment income.[1] Note the restriction. If a company carries on two or more distinct trades, the loss on one trade can only be set off against the future profits of that trade and not of the other trades that the company may carry on. If there are major changes in the nature of and ownership of the business the right of set-off may be lost.

Finance Act 1971 section 42 and Finance Act 1972 section 67 That part of the loss which is due to the application of 100 per cent first year allowances can be carried back and set off against the company's total profits of the three preceding years and tax already paid can be reclaimed.

---

[1] Income from which tax has been deducted or which attracts a tax credit.

Section 178 Terminal losses, i.e., losses in the last year of trading can be set off against the profits of the three preceding years.

Capital losses

While trading losses can be relieved against capital gains, capital losses can only be relieved by being offset against capital gains in that year or future years.

Groups of companies

The principal rules relating the groups of companies are:

1. Payment of dividends: where the paying company is 51 per cent owned by the recipient or both are 51 per cent subsidiaries of another resident company an election may be made not to pay ACT. A similar position exists where the paying company is owned by a consortium of resident companies owning at least 75 per cent of its capital.
2. ACT: where a company has surplus ACT, i.e., unrelieved ACT, for an accounting period, this can be surrendered to 51 per cent subsidiaries if they so agree. Any ACT surrendered to a subsidiary is treated as if it were ACT paid by that company in respect of distributions.
3. Group relief: trading losses of one company in a group may be set off against the profits of another, provided one is a 75 per cent subsidiary of the other or both are 75 per cent subsidiaries of a common parent company. Group relief may also be available within a consortium.

Framework of corporation tax

Assume that a company makes a profit of £100 and makes a distribution in the form of a dividend of £35. This would appear in the company's financial report as follows:

	£
Profit	100
Less: Corporation tax at 50%	50
Profit after tax	50
Dividend	35
Retained profit	15

When the dividend payment of £35 is paid the company has to pay ACT at three-sevenths of the cost of the dividend on the basis of the rates used for illustration. This would in the example amount to £15. This payment of ACT can be used to reduce the mainstream corporation tax liability for the *year in which the dividend is paid*. As far as the shareholder is concerned, he has received a dividend plus the related tax credit which covers the basic income tax. The only extra tax he may have to pay is the investment income surcharge and higher band rates. He has therefore received a dividend which for him effectively amounts to his share of the total of:

	£
Gross amount	50
Less: Basic tax at 30%	15
Net amount	35

The shareholder will suffer no additional basic income tax and if his income is such that he does not pay tax or he is a tax exempt institution, the tax credit can be reclaimed from the Inland Revenue.

The fraction of three-sevenths used in the above illustration for calculating ACT relates to a basic tax rate of 30 per cent. Where that rate is different the fraction changes, e.g., if the basic rate is 34 per cent the fraction becomes $\frac{34}{66}$.

Set-off of ACT against corporation tax

The amount of a franked payment or receipt is the amount of the payment or receipt plus the related tax credit. Franked receipts are not subject to corporation tax and may be set off against franked payments to reduce the amount of ACT payable.

The rules for setting off ACT against corporation tax are:

1. ACT is set off against the corporation tax payable for the accounting period in which the dividend is *paid*, not for the year to which it relates (although, of course, this may be the same year).
2. It can be set off against corporation tax on income and not against corporation tax on capital gains.
3. There is a limit to the set-off. When ACT plus the distribution equals the taxable income no further set-off is allowed. This means that mainstream tax will never fall below a rate representing the difference between the basic rate of income tax and the corporation tax rate.

Example of the limitation of ACT set-off

Assume that a company has a taxable income of £40 000 for the accounting period to 31 December 1977. During that accounting period it pays dividends totalling £84 000. Taking the illustrative tax rates of 30 per cent and 50 per cent, the ACT on the distribution is three-sevenths of £84 000 = £36 000. The dividends plus ACT exceed the taxable income and must be restricted as follows—£28 000 dividend plus £12 000 ACT = £40 000. The offset of ACT is therefore restricted to £12 000 and the mainstream tax payment is 50 per cent of £40 000 = £20 000, less £12 000 ACT set-off, leaving £8000 to be paid.

Surplus ACT

ACT which cannot be relieved against the mainstream corporation tax payment can be treated in two ways.

1. It can be carried back and set off against the mainstream corporation tax on the income of accounting periods beginning within the two years preceding that period.
2. It can be carried forward and set off against mainstream corporation tax in succeeding accounting periods.

However, where there are major changes in the nature and ownership of the company the carry forward may be restricted.

ACT return

Once a quarter, an ACT return must be made to the Inland Revenue which shows:

1. Franked payments made.
2. Franked income received.
3. Items where it is uncertain as to whether the distribution is a qualifying one.
4. The amount of ACT payable.

Repayment of ACT may be made where franked income is received and ACT has already been paid in the same accounting period.

Dividend warrants

Dividend warrants must show the dividend paid and the amount of the tax credit.

Small companies

Where the profits of a company for an accounting period of a year do not exceed £30 000 the rate of corporation tax is 10 per cent less than the normal rate, i.e., if the normal rate is 50 per cent the small company rate would be 40 per cent. This reduced rate does not apply to capital gains. Where the profits are over £30 000 but less than £50 000 there is marginal relief and the full corporation tax rate is only paid after the higher figure is reached.

Close companies

What is a close company?

A company cannot be close where:

1. The public own 35 per cent of the voting power and the company's shares are quoted and dealt in on a UK stock exchange.
2. It is a subsidiary of a non-close company.
3. It is a non-resident company.

Where the above exclusions do not apply then the company is close if:

1. It is controlled by five or fewer participators.

2. It is controlled by participators who are directors.
3. More than 50 per cent of the income or assets is attributable to five or fewer participators.

What is a participator?

In defining a participator the shareholding and other rights of the individual must be taken together with those of:
—Nominees for him.
—Any company which he or associates controls.
—His spouse.
—Any ancestors and descendents, brothers or sisters.
—Any partners.
—Any trustees of a settlement made by him.
—Any trusts in which he has an interest.

Effect of close company status

Where a company is close then:
1. Distributions to shareholders must reach certain standards.
2. Certain payments and benefits accruing to participators are treated as distributions and are not allowable as deductions in computing profits. These include
   (a) benefits or facilities to people other than directors or employees;
   (b) loan interest in excess of prescribed rates.
3. Loans to participators and associates attract ACT in the same way as they would if they were dividends. When the loan is repaid, the ACT is refunded.

Apportionment

Where the distributions do not meet the relevant standard the income of the company can be apportioned to the shareholders and they are then taxed on the basis that the company had in fact made the required distribution on the last day of its accounting period.

The standard The 'relevant income' or standard cannot be more than 50 per cent of distributable income where distributable income is defined as:
—The amount on which the company has to pay corporation tax *less* the corporation tax payable and any capital gains and related tax. The amount may be further adjusted for franked investment income and relief given for management expenses.
This requirement to distribute 50 per cent of distributable income is a maximum and is modified if the company needs to retain more of its income to finance its current requirements and any requirements which may be necessary or advisable for the maintenance and development of that business.

No apportionment will be made if the excess of the standard over the actual distribution is less than £1000. Distributions in this context include:
—Dividends declared in respect of the period and paid within a reasonable time after it.
—Loan interest in excess of prescribed rates.
—Expenses of providing benefits to participators.

Small companies

Where the trading or estate income is less than £5000 there will be no apportionment. Between £5000 and £15 000 the income is reduced by a half of the difference between the income and £15 000, and the 50 per cent distribution rule applies to the lower figure.

Requirements of the business

The requirements of the business which may be used to reduce the relevant income to less than 50 per cent of distributable income include both current and future requirements. They cannot include:
1. Expenditure on acquiring the original business or loans incurred in acquiring it.
2. Redemption of share capital and payment of debts incurred for inadequate consideration.
3. Artificial transactions.

Investment companies

The relevant income is the distributable income less the smaller of:
1. 10 per cent of estate or trading income.
2. £500.

Clearances

A close company (other than one with only investment income) can require the Inspector of Taxes to state whether or not he proposes to make an apportionment. The procedure is as follows:
1. The company submits the accounts adopted at the annual general meeting, the directors' report, and any other information thought fit.
2. Within three months of receipt the Inspector may call for any further information that he requires.
3. Within three months of the original application, or the receipt of any additional information requested, the Inspector must notify the company whether or not he proposes to make an apportionment.

No apportionment can be made unless the Inspector intimates his intention to do so within the stipulated time, or if misleading or inaccurate information is provided, or if the company ceases to carry on its main activity or goes into liquidation within 12 months after the end of the accounting period.

Effects of apportionment on personal tax

The sum apportioned to an individual is to be treated as:
1. Income received by him on the last day of the accounting period.
2. The top slice of his total income.

Recoupment of apportionment

Where distributions in later years exceed the relevant income, the persons who have had income apportioned to them can have its effect reversed to the extent of such excess. Since the effect of an apportionment can be reversed by paying a higher dividend in a later year there is some merit in adopting a policy of determining distributions in the light of the needs of the company and its owners, and if the company is later unable to justify its distribution policy with the result that an apportionment is made, this can be adjusted by increasing a subsequent dividend. This may be several years later, as the apportionment is only reviewed at three-year intervals by the Inspector of Taxes.

Tax planning in small companies

Directors should carefully consider the interplay between income tax, corporation tax and capital gains tax where they and their families own the company and no outside interests need to be considered. There can be no general rule since the tax position of each company and its directors can be quite different. However, there are some matters on which general guidelines can be provided.

The difference between personal tax rates and corporation tax rates should be considered. In general, it is better to increase directors' remuneration, thus reducing the company's income to the point where the marginal rate of tax paid by the director is the same as the rate of corporation tax. For example, where the small company corporation tax rate is 42 per cent it is better to distribute the company's income as extra directors' fees if the directors would only be taxed at, say, 38 per cent. Even if the directors' tax rate is higher than 42 per cent, it may be better to pay out extra directors' fees since profits retained in the business and subsequently distributed as dividends would be exposed to liability for the investment income surcharge, or if the business is sold would increase the asset value and therefore the potential liability to capital gains tax.

If the company requires all its earnings to finance growth, it can still follow the guideline set out above. In this situation the additional directors' remuneration paid out would have to be loaned back to the company. The advantage of this process is that if the directors wish to take money out of the company it merely repays some or all of the monies loaned to it by the directors, whereas if it is left in the company as undistributed profits a distribution would have to be made which would attract ACT and possibly further tax consequences in the hands of the director.

The distribution of additional directors' remuneration may also be used to reduce the income of the company to the point where it can take advantage of lower rates of tax for small companies and also minimize the possibility of an apportionment being made.

The ownership of the fixed assets to be used by the company is a further matter which should be considered, particularly land and buildings. Capital gains made by a company are still taxed twice—once in the hands of the company and again when the gain is distributed to the shareholders or, if this is not done, the potential higher capital gains tax liability when the shareholder disposes of his interest in the company. If, however, the major shareholders or the directors hold the asset personally then any gain that might arise on its disposal would be taxed once only at the personal rate of capital gains tax (which is one half of the marginal rate of income tax or 30 per cent, whichever is the lower).

Capital gains tax

Any person, partnership, company, etc., resident or ordinarily resident in the UK is liable to capital gains tax on the disposal of an asset anywhere in the world (unless not domiciled in the UK, when only gains remitted to this country are taxable). Certain assets are exempt from the tax, the principal items being:
—Private motor cars.
—Main private residence.
—British Government securities held for more than one year.
—Sales of chattels for £1000 or less.
If the total disposals for the year are less than £1000 they are exempted from the tax.

Disposal of an asset includes not only outright sale, but also the gift of an asset, and its destruction, e.g., by fire. Gifts or sales to one's wife are not treated as a disposal but when finally disposed of the gain is calculated by reference to the orginal cost. On death there is deemed to be a disposal of all assets held, but at the present time no capital gains tax is payable.

Capital losses

Any loss arising from a disposal can be set off against any gains for that year and against any net gains of husband or wife. Any remaining unrelieved loss can be carried forward and set off against gains arising in future years.

Assets owned on 6 April 1965

Assets other than quoted shares and securities held on 6 April 1965 when sold will have the gain 'time apportioned', i.e., the gain will be assumed to have accrued evenly over the whole period it was owned and only the gain accruing after 6 April 1965 is taxable. Alternatively the taxpayer can elect within two years after the end of the tax year in which the disposal was made to substitute 6 April 1965 market value for the time adjusted value.

Replacement of business assets

Sales of any assets used in a business are liable to capital gains tax. However, if additional business assets are purchased within the year preceding and three years after the sale, the gain can be 'rolled over' on to the new assets acquired. The effect of rolling over the gain is that the amount of the gain is deducted from the cost of the new assets, thus effectively increasing the gain on their disposal. The roll-over process can, however, be repeated when they come to be sold.

Business retirement relief

A person over 65 years of age who disposes of all or part of a business he has owned for the last 10 years or shares in a trading company which is 'family owned' for the last 10 years, is exempt from capital gains tax on the first £20 000 of any gain. A family-owned company is one where the taxpayer has 25 per cent of the voting rights, or his immediate family has at least 75 per cent of those rights including at least 10 per cent held by the taxpayer himself.

Rates of tax

The rate of capital gains tax for the individual is 30 per cent or, if lower, one half of the gain taxed at the marginal rate of income tax. In effect, one half of the gain is added to the income for the year and taxed as though it was income.

The capital gains of companies are subject to corporation tax but before being added to other profits a fraction of the gain is deducted. At the present time (1976) this fraction is eleven twenty-sixths.

Capital transfer tax

Capital transfer tax is a tax on cumulative gifts over one's lifetime and at death. If the cumulative total of such gifts is more than £15 000 then tax will be payable. Unless this threshold is raised most people are likely to fall into the net at some time. Gifts between husband and wife are exempt.

Exemptions

Since it is a tax on capital transfers, gifts out of income are not taxable provided that they would not reduce the donor's standard of living. Individual gifts of up to £100 *and* gifts not exceeding £2000 per year are exempt, as are gifts of up to £5000 on marriage

Rates of tax

Each 'slice' of total gifts is subject to a different rate. For example, for lifetime gifts the first £5000 above the £15 000 threshold is taxed at 5 per cent and the £120 000 to £150 000 slice is taxed at 35 per cent. The rate of tax on gifts at death is higher. For example, the rate for the last illustration is 55 per cent on gifts at death.

The rate of tax can be misunderstood since if one gives away £100 000 the tax is not at the £100 000 rate but the rate appropriate to a gift which, after tax, would produce £100 000. To give away £100 000 during one's lifetime would attract CTT of £19 483. The gift is assumed to be one of £119 483 on which tax of £19 483 would be due. Only if the recipient of the gift assumes liability for paying the tax would it be computed on the actual amount of the gift. In the case of gifts of business assets a person receiving a gift and assuming the liability for CTT can spread the payment over eight annual instalments. (Business assets are subject to a percentage reduction for CTT purposes.)

While the fact that lifetime gifts are taxed at a lower rate than gifts on death may indicate that one's assets should be given away during one's life, it must be remembered that such a gift is a disposal for capital gains tax purposes. Any gain on the assets given away would be subject to capital gains tax and this is not deductible from value of the asset for CTT, whereas capital gains arising at death are not taxed. There is also the general proposition that it is better to pay taxes later rather than earlier.

The Conservative Party is pledged to repeal CTT in its present form, which adds to the uncertainties as to how to plan one's affairs. There are, however, one or two general points that can be made:

—Husbands and wives should divide total assets equally between them. For example, if total assets are £30 000 all held by one partner then CTT would be payable by that partner on £15 000 (the first £15 000 being exempt). On the other hand if each spouse holds £15 000 and each gives their assets away to third parties the whole amount is exempt.

—The maximum advantage should be taken of the small gifts exemptions year by year. Husband and wife can each give away £2000 per year and the under-used exemption in one year can be carried forward to the next year.

5.

Sources of capital

It is almost inevitable that at some time directors will be involved in decisions related to raising new funds to finance the company. Such decisions can have an important influence on its long-term viability and directors should be aware of the characteristics of each source of funds. In particular, the term for which the funds are available, i.e., whether they are short term or long term, and the effect that using a particular source may have on the return to shareholders and the risk of business failure must be seriously considered. This chapter is concerned with a description of the sources of capital that may be available, long term and short term. Subsequent chapters will deal with the analysis of the decision from the corporate viability and return to shareholder points of view.

Long-term funds: shareholders' funds

Issued share capital is the most permanent source of capital and the one that carries the least risk of business failure since share capital does not need to be repaid (indeed it is illegal to do so without the sanction of the courts), and the shareholders have no absolute right to dividends. In planning the use to be made of share capital, consideration should be given to the rights which attach to different classes of share and which is the most appropriate for the company's needs, as well as to the amount which should be raised in this way.

The amount of share capital which can be issued is set out in the memorandum of association of the company. The directors should consider whether the amount authorized by the memorandum is adequate for the company's needs and, if not, an extraordinary general meeting of shareholders should be called to revise the authorized amount in the light of the company's present and future needs. The rights which attach to different classes of share are determined by the company and are set out in its articles of association.

The distinction between the different classes of share is based upon the way in which three rights are allocated between the different classes:
1. The right to income: the income attributable to the shareholders can be distributed between different classes of shares in any way that the company desires.

2. The right to repayment on liquidation: when the claims of all creditors
have been met the remaining assets can be distributed between the different
classes in a manner determined by the company.

3. The right to vote.

Each company devises its own classes of share, but in practice they tend to
follow a similar pattern with similar rights attaching to the same class of
share in different companies. The principal classes likely to be used are dealt
with below.

Preference shares

This class has a prior right to dividends up to a fixed rate, e.g., a holder of a
5 per cent preference share would be entitled to a dividend which must be
5 per cent before anything can be paid to other classes, e.g., ordinary shareholders. The shares can be either cumulative or non-cumulative. In the latter
case, if the dividend is not paid in any year it is lost for ever to the shareholder,
whereas if it is cumulative it accumulates until the company is in a position
to pay it.

When the company goes into liquidation the preference shareholder would
receive repayment of his capital or a stated sum, before any payment could
be made to other shareholders. Usually the preference shareholder has no
right to vote unless his dividend is in arrears.

In some cases the company might want the right to redeem preference
shares. If this is so a class of redeemable preference shares could be issued
which give the company the right to redeem them on the terms stated in the
articles. To exercise this right the company must either accumulate an
equivalent amount of undistributed profits and gains and put them aside
in a 'capital redemption reserve fund' which has the characteristics of issued
capital, or make the redemption from the proceeds of a new issue of capital.

Ordinary shares

Ordinary shares are normally entitled to the residual profits and assets after
the claims of all other classes of share have been met. It is the class of share
in which the voting control of the company usually lies.

Other classes of share may be issued. Participating preference shares and
preferred ordinary shares, as their names imply, have similar rights to income
as preference shares but in addition they can participate in the distribution
of earnings above stated levels. Deferred or founder's shares are essentially
ordinary shares but their right to income is suspended until some specified
event occurs, such as earnings exceeding a certain level or ordinary dividends
exceeding a given rate.

It is the responsibility of the directors in conjunction with their financial
advisers to decide what attributes are appropriate for the various classes of
share the company may issue. As for the investing public, their major interest
is in ordinary shares.

Characteristics of share capital

Share capital of all classes has two major characteristics which must be considered when planning the overall capital structure.

1. There are no repayment requirements for share capital, with the exception of redeemable preference shares already noted.
2. There is no obligation to pay dividends. Before making any distribution to shareholders the directors would have to consider the needs of the business. The prerequisites for a dividend to be paid are, first, that there should be realized profits out of which the dividend can be paid (this is a legal requirement) and, second, the directors must recommend the dividend. They are therefore discretionary payments and there is no guarantee that even preference shareholders will receive a dividend, even if the company has made a profit in the period.

New issues of share capital

Private and non-quoted public companies The private and non-quoted public company seeking to raise capital through the issue of shares can do so either from its existing shareholders or from personal contacts and business associates who may be prevailed upon to back the company. Existing shareholders may already have their resources tied up in the company and may not be able to provide further finance. Bringing in new shareholders may affect the control exercised by existing shareholders and future decisions made would have to take into account the interests of the new shareholders—there must be no oppression of minority shareholders or the courts may be asked to intervene. Where the company is of a size that it may be able to obtain a stock exchange quotation in the foreseeable future it may be able to place shares privately with an institution which will then guide it on the path to a quotation if desired. Shares must not be offered to the public at large as there are a number of prerequisites for this to take place, such as publishing a prospectus, and in any case this is not a course of action open to the private company.

Quoted companies New issues of share capital can be effected in one of three ways:

1. A public issue by way of offer for sale to the public: this requires a full prospectus to be prepared and advertised in at least two leading London newspapers. The cost of advertising and the administrative costs of the issue make this relatively expensive for the small quoted company.
2. A rights issue to existing shareholders: the new shares are offered to the existing shareholders in proportion to their existing holdings by means of a provisional letter of allotment. The individual shareholders may accept the offer contained in the letter of allotment and subscribe for the new shares, or they may renounce their rights in favour of someone else, either

as a gift or by a sale through the market. Since the new shares will normally be offered to the shareholders at a price less than the pre-issue market price, the post-issue market price of the shares will be less than before the issue.

3. Private placing: the new shares are placed directly with institutional investors, or with members of the stock exchange for subsequent marketing.

When considering the issue of new shares the company will most likely call upon the services of a member of the Issuing Houses Association, whose members include the leading firms handling this type of business. They can advise on the method to adopt, the timing of the issue, and on the law and practice governing issues. After satisfying themselves that the amount of capital is reasonable and is obtainable on suitable terms and conditions, the issuing house takes on the responsibility for raising the funds required.

Retained profit

Undistributed profits and gains automatically add to the long-term funds used in the business. Year by year the directors must decide upon the way the company's earnings are to be divided between dividends and amounts to be retained in the business. The elements of the dividend policy decision are discussed in a later chapter.

Long-term borrowing

A company may meet some of its capital needs by borrowing money on a long-term basis. Such borrowing may be in the form of:

—A mortgage on the company's premises.

—A debenture which is secured by a fixed and/or floating charge on the company's assets.

—Other loans which are secured on the company's assets.

—Unsecured loans.

—Subordinated loans. These rank after creditors and are usually issued to shareholders.

In contrast to share capital, loan capital must be repaid at specified dates; interest must be paid at specific intervals, usually half yearly; and there may be other stipulations which the company must observe, such as to maintain a certain asset cover for the loan. If the company fails in any of these commitments to the lender(s) they have the right either to have the loan repaid immediately or to appoint a receiver who takes over the assets charged. The risk characteristics are therefore very different from share capital.

The small company will usually arrange a loan directly with the lender or through the intermediary of a solicitor or accountant. Large companies may divide the loan into units in very much the same way as share capital is divided into shares, and market them in one of the ways outlined previously for new share issues. Such issues almost invariably carry a stock exchange quotation and they are bought and sold in the same manner as shares. There would be difficulty in a large body of loanstockholders exercising their rights under the terms of the loan and therefore a trustee (usually one of the major banks or insurance companies) is appointed who exercises that function on behalf of the stockholders.

Institutions which are prepared to lend money on a long-term basis include insurance companies, pension funds and finance companies. In the case of direct loans to a company, the amount of the loan would normally have to be in excess of £50 000. The loan may be repayable by instalments over a specified period, by the proceeds of an endowment insurance policy, or by establishing a sinking fund to provide a lump sum repayment at the end of the loan period. Freehold property is the most favourably regarded security for a loan and an insurance company would expect to receive all the insurance business from the borrower.

Other institutions which may be prepared to lend money long-term include building societies, which may lend up to 75 per cent of the valuation of property. They are, however, limited by law in the amounts that they can lend to companies and as to the maximum amount of individual loans. Generally there is a reluctance to lend on business properties. Trading connections can sometimes be prevailed upon to lend money, for example breweries and petroleum companies may offer finance to the owner of an outlet on advantageous terms. Such contractual arrangements normally restrict the retailer's choice of brands since the purpose in offering loans in this way is primarily to secure the exclusive sale of the lender's products.

Convertible loans

Convertible loans offer the lender the right to convert his loan into ordinary shares of the company. For example, the terms of the loan may give the lender the right to convert the loan into ordinary shares on 30 June in each of the years 1978, 1979, and 1980, at the following rates:
1978—100 ordinary shares per £100 nominal of loan stock,
1979—98 ordinary shares per £100 nominal of loan stock,
1980—95 ordinary shares per £100 nominal of loan stock.
Convertible loans tend to be valued at the appropriate rate for an equivalent normal loan when the ordinary share price is below the equivalent conversion price. But when the ordinary share price moves above that value, the loan stock will tend to be valued as though it was converted into ordinary shares.

Convertible loans can be useful when raising more equity capital might be difficult because of low share price or the inability of earnings to guarantee increased dividends. In such a situation they might be offered to shareholders on a rights basis or to the public. As a loan it guarantees a level of return in the form of interest and at the same time enables the holder to participate in any growth in the ordinary share price.

Warrants

The price which can be obtained from the sale of new long-term securities of a company can be increased at no cash outlay to the company by attaching warrants to the issue. The warrant enables the holder to purchase new ordinary shares in the future at a favourable fixed price.

Both convertible loans and warrants may require the issue of new equity in the future and therefore the dilution effect that this can have must be taken account of in long-term financial planning.

Long-term funds from specialist financial institutions

Over the years a number of specialist institutions have been established with a view to meeting capital needs of firms which cannot be met from other sources.

Finance for industry (FFI)

Finance for Industry was established in 1975 to invigorate and coordinate two existing lending institutions, the Industrial and Commercial Finance Corporation (ICFC) and the Finance Corporation for Industry (FCI) both founded in 1945. The group is 85 per cent owned by the major banks with the remaining 15 per cent owned by the Bank of England.

ICFC (91 Waterloo Road, London SE1 8XP)

The role of ICFC is to provide long-term finance from £5000 to £1m or more to smaller firms which find it difficult to raise new capital from banks or by a public issue. The rate of interest is fixed for the period of the loan and repayments can be spread over periods of up to 20 years. As a condition of lending money ICFC will probably require a part of the ordinary shares to be made available to it so that it can participate in the capital growth that its lending activities supports. At the same time there is considerable flexibility in tailoring the financial package to the real needs of the client company. ICFC also administers in the UK special loans to small companies in development areas provided by the European Investment Bank as part of the EEC regional policies.

ICFC is more than just a lending institution. Before agreeing to lend money it carries out an extensive appraisal of the company's operations and management as well as its financial state so that it can be satisfied that the company is a sound investment. It is more directly involved with its clients than most other lenders and may provide advisory services where needed. If a client company plans to obtain a stock exchange quotation, ICFC will 'nurse' the company in that direction and act as the issuing house to the subsequent public offer.

FCI (4 Bread Street, London EC4)

Established at the same time as ICFC, FCI is designed for the larger company requiring funds in excess of £250 000 which cannot be satisfied from other sources. Since the most secure uses of new capital are likely to be financed from conventional sources, those left to be financed by FCI are likely to carry more than an ordinary degree of risk. Like ICFC it may require the allotment to it of ordinary shares or the right to convert part of the loan into ordinary shares.

Estate Duty Investment Trust Ltd (EDITH) (91 Waterloo Road, London SE1 8XP)
The death of the principal shareholder in a family company poses serious problems in the light of capital transfer tax. Whether CTT is borne by the deceased's estate or by the recipient of the estate, if there are no other assets from which the tax can be paid the drain of liquid resources and the necessity of selling shares to meet the tax can put at risk the continuity, control and ownership of the company. The cash drain can be mitigated to some extent if the recipient pays the tax and exercises the right to pay CTT in instalments over eight years. This, however, only applies to transfers of up to £250 000.

EDITH was established in 1953 by a group of insurance companies and investment trusts to relieve the immediate needs of paying estate duty and now CTT, and enabling the company to continue as a separate entity under the same control. This it achieves by taking up a minority interest in the share capital of the company concerned and holding it as an investment on a long-term basis. EDITH is managed by ICFC and offers services similar to the latter and together with the other shareholders will make shares available to the market if the company seeks a stock exchange quotation. Otherwise it does not interfere in the day-to-day management of the company.

Certain other institutions provide finance for the payment of CTT. These include:
—Charterhouse Group Ltd.
—Industrial Finance and Investment Corporation Ltd.
—Private Enterprise Investment Company Ltd.
—Safeguard Industrial Investment Ltd.

Technical Development Capital Ltd (TDC) (7 Copthall Avenue, London EC2)
TDC is another institution whose management is in the hands of ICFC. Its share capital is in the hands of a number of UK and overseas insurance companies, merchant banks, and other institutions. Its function is to try and overcome the problems of the inventor or innovator who lacks the capital to exploit his ideas commercially. The development or innovation must have passed the initial research stage so that it can be demonstrated that it will work and can be patented, but is not being produced on a commercial basis because of lack of capital.

Unlike the institutions already mentioned, TDC financial aid is not a permanent investment. It concentrates its support during the period necessary to bring the invention to a profitable stage and thereafter will try and sell all or most of its interest. This it may do by selling it back to the inventor or to some other institution, or by participating in a public offer of shares. This intent to divest itself of its interests when the profitable stage is reached will not be exercised in a way that would harm the original investors' interests.

Other institutions which deal with similar requirements or with 'start-up' situations include:
—European Business Development Ltd.
—Small Business Capital Fund Ltd.
—Midland Montague Industrial Finance Ltd.
—County Bank Ltd.
—Charterhouse Group.
—Hambros Bank.

National Research and Development Corporation (NRDC) (Kingsgate House, 66 Victoria Street, London SW1)
NRDC is not concerned with the commercial exploitation of inventions but can help in one of two ways. It may provide one half of the development costs of an invention and recoup its outlay by imposing a royalty on the sales of the product, or it can fund all of the development costs and recoup its outlay by selling a licence to a commercial firm and taking one half of the royalties.

Council for Small Industries in Rural Areas (CoSIRA) (35 Camp Road, Wimbledon Common, London SW19 4UP)
CoSIRA provides financial, technical and managerial support to firms in rural areas and small towns. The size of the loan can range from £250 to £30 000. Similar facilities are available in Scotland.

Single Industry Financial Institutions
There are a number of specialist financial institutions which are designed to serve the needs of a single industry. Among these are:
—The Agricultural Mortgage Corporation Ltd (for England and Wales) and the Scottish Agricultural Securities Corporation Ltd. These organizations provide loans against first mortgages on agricultural land and buildings, and for the carrying out of improvements to such properties. Loans are usually limited to two-thirds of the estimated value of the property and the rate of interest may be fixed or floating, i.e., it varies with the market rate of interest in much the same way as a building society's rate fluctuates.
—Ship Mortgage Finance Co. Ltd. SMFC helps British shipowners through the provision of finance on completed ships built in UK shipyards. Loans are made on the security of a first mortgage on the vessels concerned.
—National Film Finance Corporation Ltd. Financed by the government and

financial institutions, it is now required to be self-supporting and has only limited resources available.

Merchant banks and other financial institutions

Merchant banks and other financial institutions may provide finance directly to companies or put together financing packages designed to meet specific needr. They may have access not only to funds within the UK but also overseas sources of funds, such as loans on the Eurocurrency market. Institutions include:

—Hambros Bank Ltd, 51 Bishopsgate, London EC2P 2AA. (£50 000 upwards in the form of equity and loan capital to small- and medium-sized companies.)

—Slater, Walker Developments Ltd, 30 St Paul's Churchyard, London EC4M 8DA. (Medium-term loans and equity capital.)

—County Bank Ltd (National Westminster Bank Group), 11 Old Broad Street, London EC2N 1BB.

—National and Commercial Development Capital Ltd (National and Commercial Banking Group), 34 Nicholas Lane, London EC4P 4HX. (£100 000 upwards for companies capable of earning pre-tax profits in excess of £100 000.)

We shall now move on to consider sources of short-term funds.

Short-term funds: bank credit

Unlike their continental and Japanese counterparts, UK banks do not normally provide long-term finance but confine the majority of their lending activities to financing the short-term requirements of their customers. It is the classic illustration of the principle that short-term funds should only be used to finance short-term uses. The funds loaned by the banks are monies deposited by the bank's customers which are repayable on demand or at very short notice and they are loaned to customers normally on the basis that they are repayable on demand. This basic 'repayable on demand' principle is somewhat mitigated in practice. The usual procedure for negotiating bank credit is for the customer to agree an overdraft limit with the bank for the coming year or other period and the customer can rely on this facility being available for that period of time provided the terms and conditions set by the bank are observed. At the end of the agreed period the bank and its customer meet to review the situation and agree facilities and terms for the following period. In appropriate cases, e.g., temporary finance for the acquisition of an asset, the bank may make a direct loan repayable in instalments over a relatively short period.

Directors should appreciate the point of view of the bank manager in reaching a decision to lend money. It is not the bank's money which is being lent but money belonging to other customers. The bank is effectively taking all the risk of default for what is a very small return. The bank manager will therefore look very closely at the borrowers integrity, his ability to generate funds to repay the loan (ideally it should be self liquidating), and the security for the loan in case of default.

Illustrations of self-liquidating loans are:

—Loans to meet seasonal peaks of demand where the borrowing to support the peak demand is repaid from the flow back of funds as the level of business declines to the trough.

—Finance to enable the company to accept a major order, the loan being repaid from the sales proceeds.

—A bridging loan to cover the period of time between the company making a major outlay for an asset and raising the finance for it, or when, for example, a building is purchased and the purchase price is to be financed by the sale of a building already owned, to cover the period between the purchase of the new and the receipt of the sales proceeds from the old building.

Banks do, however, modify the self-liquidating principle in practice. Providing a customer's financial state of affairs is satisfactory, the bank is likely to renew year-by-year facilities required to meet a company's working capital needs.

The security may be provided by a potential or actual charge on the assets of the company. When lending to well-established customers to meet working capital needs the bank may not require any formal security, but rely on the creditworthiness of the company. The extent to which the company has charged its assets as security for other loans has a major influence, in that it reduces the asset cover for bank lending. In other cases the bank may require a formal charge on the company's assets and in the case of smaller companies may require directors or other parties to provide personal guarantees to the bank. Where a company holds exceptionally high levels of stocks of materials it may be able to arrange bank finance for the stocks by hypothecation of the stocks. The stocks are held in bond and form the security for the loan. The managers of the bonded warehouse control all movements in and out of the store and such movements are notified to the bank.

Directors should consider the strategy to be adopted towards relations with the bank. The goodwill of the bank can be of inestimable value to a company and everything should be done to foster the best of relations. When the bank manager is considering a loan proposal he is greatly assisted if he is already in possession of the fullest information about the company, its business, and its management.

Directors should formulate a long-term strategy irrespective of whether they need funds at the present time or not so that the foundations are laid for when the need to borrow arises. From time to time the bank manager should be invited to see what the company is doing and to meet its directors and senior officials. He should be informed of major developments and presented with the annual report. All of this should provide a vital framework of reference for him to use should the need to arrange bank credit arise.

The short-term strategy for negotiating a particular loan requirement must also be considered. The financial information about the company should be brought up to date if necessary, and financial data to support the loan application prepared. This would include:

—A statement as to why the facility is required.

—Other relevant statements of the company's state of affairs, such as the value of debtors, orders in hand, etc.

—A cash budget showing the likely cash flows over the period of the loan. This should show how the amount required has been arrived at and how it is to be repaid.

Trade credit

The use of short-term credit provided by suppliers can make a useful contribution towards reducing the working capital needs of a company. Properly controlled within the constraints of liquidity requirements, it should form part of the overall financing strategy. The excessive use of trade credit can, however, be dangerous. A company which finds it difficult to raise long-term capital, and as a consequence uses trade credit as a substitute for long-term funds, is much more at risk of failure than a company which has been financed by the appropriate amount of long-term funds.

Trade credit is often thought of as being cost free since no interest or dividends are payable for its use. To some extent this is true, particularly if the use made of such credit is kept within the supplier's credit terms. If credit terms are exceeded, however, costs can be incurred.

Loss of cash discounts or incurring interest costs The cost of losing cash discounts can be high. For example, if through taking an extra month's credit a $2\frac{1}{2}$ per cent cash discount is lost this is effectively paying 30 per cent on an annual basis for the use of that money.

Interruption of supplies If a company persistently delays payment to creditors some of them may retaliate by withholding supplies, or, where there are bottlenecks in deliveries, giving priority to prompt payers. The cost of production or delivery delays due to such actions is rarely highlighted but nevertheless can be very heavy.

Downgrading of credit rating Credit rating agencies receive reports from certain suppliers as to promptness of payment. If reports begin to reflect a slowing-down of payments this is reflected in the credit rating agencies reports to its own clients. Other suppliers may through an analysis of the company's accounts detect a lengthening of the payment period.

Instalment credit, hire purchase, and leasing

A company may reduce the pressure on finance by using instalment credit, hire purchase or leasing instead of buying the asset outright.

Instalment credit The company acquires the ownership of the asset but pays the cost in instalments over a period of time.

Hire purchase The company hires the asset over an agreed period of time paying a rental for its use. At the end of the agreement period ownership passes to the hirer on the payment of a nominal sum. Although technically the asset does not become the property of the hirer until the end of the agreement, for accounting purposes it is usual to treat the asset as owned by the company and show the amount outstanding under the agreement as a liability.

Leasing The asset is never owned by the lessee. It merely pays an annual rental for its use over a given period. If it wishes to retain the asset after that period this can usually be done on payment of a nominal rental. As the asset is never owned, capital allowances cannot be claimed for it since they accrue to the leasing company and the rental should reflect this fact. The rental payments are fully deductible for tax purposes and the amount of such payments must be disclosed separately in the financial report.

Invoice factoring and discounting

Both forms are designed to reduce the amount of capital locked up in debtors. The principal difference between the two forms is that with the discounting method the selling company collects the amounts due from its customers in the normal way and accounts for it to the finance company which has discounted the invoices, whereas with factoring the finance house assumes responsibility for collecting the amounts due from customers. Before considering proposals to use this source of finance directors should consider the following problems.

1. Will a separate sales company be required? (This may increase administrative costs.)
2. Does the finance company have recourse against the selling company for any bad debts?
3. What degree of credit control will the finance company exercise?

This can be a fairly expensive source of capital, but when other less expensive sources have been exhausted it may prove useful in enabling a business to expand. The major banks have subsidiaries operating in this field and there are a number owned by finance houses.

Bill finance

A bill of exchange is an unconditional order in writing addressed to a person requiring him to pay on demand or at a fixed or determinable future time a sum of money to or to the order of a specified person or bearer (a cheque is a bill of exchange payable on demand). When used to finance the movement of goods the seller of the goods draws a bill of exchange on the purchaser payable at, say, 90 days after sight for the value of the goods. The purchaser 'accepts' the bill by writing 'accepted' on the face of it and signing and dating it. The bill is then a contract between the parties quite independent of the contract of sale of the goods, and can be sold by the seller of the goods for a sum close to its face value. This difference represents interest earned by the person who advanced the money against the bill. The seller of the goods can thus obtain cash for them close to the date of the sale and the purchaser does not have to pay for them for 90 days.

While bills of exchange are used mainly in overseas trade they are used to some extent in inland trade. They are also used sometimes to secure repayment of loans from finance companies, the borrower accepting a series of bills of exchange each with a different maturity date.

The cost of discounting a bill depends on the financial standing of the parties to the bill. An acceptor of a bill could range from a multi-national corporation to a relatively unknown company or individual trader. This can be overcome by arranging for a bank or an accepting house to issue a letter of credit to the seller who can then draw the bill of exchange on the bank and not the purchaser for up to the amount of and within the terms of the letter of credit. The institution then assumes the responsibility for payment of the bill on maturity and as it bears a well known name the cost of discounting will be less.

Financing exports

Where sales are made to overseas customers, directors should give consideration to a number of factors including:
—The necessity of extending lengthy credit to win an overseas order, particularly in the case of capital goods.
—The usual commercial risks of the customer defaulting on payment.
—The political risks, such as cancellation of import licences, imposition of exchange control restrictions, outbreak of war or revolution, etc.
While a number of institutions provide cover against commercial risks, the insurance of both commercial and political risks is the province of the Export Credit Guarantee Department (Aldermanbury House, Aldermanbury, London EC2P 2EL). The premiums charged depend upon the underlying risks. Such cover is usually an essential condition for a financial institution to provide credit facilities for such business.

For short-term export credit a bank overdraft is the cheapest and when covered by an ECGD guarantee the interest cost is usually $\frac{1}{2}$ per cent above base rate for up to two years and at a fixed rate for two to five years with a minimum of seven per cent. The bill of exchange referred to above is also a favourite medium for financing exports. The usual procedure is for the overseas buyer to arrange through his bank for the London office (or representative) of that bank to issue an irrevocable letter of credit. This is an undertaking by the overseas bank to accept a bill of exchange drawn on it against the delivery of the document of title to the goods, e.g. the bill of lading, which conform to the terms of the letter of credit. The seller can then discount the accepted bill in the usual way.

For medium-term finance of up to five years, bank facilities may be used supported by the ECGD guarantee, or the services of institutions such as Exporters Refinance Corporation, Commercial Export Credit Company, or Amstel Finance AG who advance cash against shipments. Longer-term finance may depend upon whether the goods are part of a financial aid scheme, in which case the exporter receives payment from the financing agency which itself extends credit to the customer, or whether it is a direct sale. In the latter case the deal will usually be handled by a merchant bank which arranges ECGD cover and the finance from other banks.

Credit insurance

While not strictly a source of finance, the insurance of book debts against the risk of default may enhance the willingness of banks and other institutions to finance debtors. Directors should also give consideration to the desirability of insuring debts to prevent undue losses.

A company's trading activity can range from small sales to a very large number of customers to one with a very large sales value to each of a small number of customers. In the former case insurance against bad debts would not be desirable since the company is effectively self insured through its wide spread of risks. In the latter case it may well be desirable to effect such insurance. Indeed, in any situation where the default of a single customer would endanger the continued existence of the company, insurance against bad debts should be effected.

The customer as a source of short-term finance

Where the relationship between the company and a major customer is substantial and continuing it may be possible to build into the trading relationship arrangements for the customer to provide materials on free issue or to finance the acquisition of fixed assets, or to provide finance to support work in progress. This is particularly useful for the smaller company which works on sub-contract for its customers.

6.

Relations with shareholders

In the present social climate directors may be excused for feeling some bewilderment as to where their primary duties lie. On the one hand is their legal duty to the shareholders on whose behalf they manage the business. On the other hand, politicians and 'social scientists' proclaim duties to employees, to the community, to customers, and to the state. Unfortunately the debate is carried on on the basis that there are inherent and fundamental conflicts between the different interests of each group, in particular between shareholders and employees. Nothing could be further from the truth. The events of the mid-1970s in the UK clearly demonstrated that companies with clear-cut financial policies designed to protect the long-term interests of the shareholders by maintaining adequate profitability and liquidity contributed far more to employee job security, to financing the state's activities and to the community at large than did those who seemed to pay scant regard to the interests of the shareholders.

The truth is that there need be no long-term conflicts between the various groups and one can go so far as to argue that all the groups have a common interest in the profitability and survival of the company. In particular the long-term interests of the shareholders can only be adequately safeguarded if the directors actively pursue policies that produce harmonious relations with employees and provide security of employment for them, that promote the right commercial relations with customers, and that do not adversely affect the environment. Employment security can only be achieved for employees through maintaining a financially healthy company, thus enabling it to have access to the capital markets to finance growth, an access which can only be secured if the company is able to offer adequate returns to investors. The community is best served by having prosperous industrial and commercial activities, irrespective of whether they are state owned or privately owned. This spurious conflict between sectional interests has been the continuing bugbear of British industry for decades. What is required is a recognition that all have a common interest in working towards a solution which must be based upon this community of interest.

For a company in the private sector there is one thing that is quite clear: if it does not offer a sufficiently attractive return to investors, whether they are lending money to the company or committing that money permanently as shareholders' funds, the ability of the company to raise the capital that it requires for growth will be severely constrained. In times of crisis, while other companies may be able to obtain institutional or public support, such a company may fail to do so and go to the wall.

The interests of the shareholders cannot be considered as something quite irrelevant to the best interests of the company. There is a strong correlation between the view that investors have of the merits of a particular company and that company's long-term viability. The policies devised by the directors should therefore be based upon safeguarding and promoting the shareholders' interests and in particular in devising the appropriate policies to ensure that values created in the company are effectively transferred as value in the hands of the shareholders. This transfer of value can only be achieved by the promotion of the company's image as an investment medium and the adoption of the right policies on matters such as dividend policy; the way that the company is financed; and on the terms of rights issues.

Dividend policy

The dividend policy decision should be based upon consideration of three major factors: the legal requirements governing the payment of dividends, the attitude of shareholders to the receipt of dividends, and the financial requirements of the company.

Legal requirements

Directors should consider the purely legal requirements for the payment of dividends and the fact that most of the recommendations of the Jenkins Committee are adopted in practice. The memorandum and articles of the company can impose further restrictions on the payment of dividends but not so as to override the legal requirements. In the following discussion the bare legal requirement and best practice should be distinguished.

1. Dividends must not be paid if the result of doing so would leave the company in a position where it would be unable to pay its debts as they became due.

2. Losses of fixed assets need not be made good as long as there is a revenue profit for the period. There is no legal requirement to make provision for depreciation of wasting assets—however, good accounting practice would require this to be done.

3. Losses of current assets in the accounting period must be made good, otherwise it cannot be said that the company has made a profit.

4. It has been held that unrealized capital profits arising from an upwards revaluation of assets could be distributed as a dividend. However, the Jenkins Committee recommended that their use in this way should be

banned although they could continue to be used to pay up a bonus issue and this is the common practice.

5. Losses made in previous accounting periods need not be made good before a dividend can be paid out of the current year's profits. The Jenkins Committee recommended the abrogation of this rule as far as losses on revenue account are concerned. The more appropriate practice in such a case would be to write down the existing capital with the sanction of the court, thus eliminating the accumulated loss. This would also have the benefit of expressing the dividend on a smaller capital base and it would make it easier for the company to raise new share capital.

6. Past profits can be used for payment of a dividend in a year in which a loss is made. Undistributed profits of previous years retain the characteristic of profits which can be distributed even if they are transferred to a separate account, such as general reserve. Only if they are used to pay up a bonus issue would they be locked in as issued capital.

7. Any realized profit on the sale of fixed assets may be treated as profit available for distribution, provided that there is an overall surplus of assets over liabilities. Accounting practice would indicate that all assets should be revalued for this purpose and the Jenkins Committee recommended that such a profit should only be distributable if the directors are satisfied that the net value of the remaining assets exceeds their book value in aggregate.

In the past the courts have held that dividends must not be paid out of capital or that they may be paid only from profits. In Flitcroft's Case in 1882 directors who created fictitious profits through crediting in the accounts debts which they knew to be bad were held to be liable to refund dividends paid on their recommendation since these had in effect amounted to an unauthorized reduction of capital.

Directors may have to consider other legal restraints when deciding on a particular dividend. In the UK two periods of dividend control by statute have been in force, the second of these lasting several years. Such dividend control has been part of a government policy to control inflation and has limited dividend increases to specified percentages. Increases in excess of the specified percentage require specific Treasury approval, e.g., when the company wishes to increase the dividend to fend off an unwelcome takeover bid. Framing a long-term dividend policy should take into account the possibility of continuing dividend control. This would argue for increasing the dividend by the maximum permitted amount each year and to take the effect on dividend yield into account when determining the number of shares and offer price in a rights issue.

Close companies are not subject to dividend control to the extent that they need to meet the minimum standard for distributions discussed on p. 41. The directors of close companies have to consider a dividend policy that meets the requirements of their cash flow and tax problems and as far as possible is within the minimum distribution. The company's own memorandum and articles of association may set out much more rigorous requirements for a dividend to be paid than those set out above. They may limit dividends to those which can be paid out of profits as distinct from capital gains, whether realized or not. The director should be conversant with the requirements relating to his own company.

Non-legal constraints

In framing a dividend policy the board should take into account the commercial considerations. For example, if the company is in a period where there is a shortage of cash it may be imprudent to pay a dividend which will make the cash position worse. Or, if retained profits are the only source of long-term capital the company can obtain, then there may be long-term growth considerations to take into account.

Declaration of dividends

The method of declaring dividends depends entirely upon the company's articles of association. In practice they have become standardized and provide that the directors recommend the dividend and an amount not exceeding that recommended can be declared by the shareholders in general meeting. Directors are usually entitled to set aside reserves out of the profits before recommending the dividend and to pay interim dividends. Control of dividends is therefore clearly in the hands of directors. Shareholders have no say in the payment of interim dividends and as far as final dividends are concerned can only reduce an amount recommended by the board.

Other matters

Since April 1973 dividends are declared as an amount per share. The directors may want to preserve the 'trustee status' of the company (trustee status enables trustees to invest part of trust funds in shares). This status may be lost if the company omits its dividend.

The shareholder and dividends

The attitude of shareholders to dividends is a rather complex matter but one which the board should consider, as those attitudes will be reflected in the market price for the company's shares. Different shareholders have different requirements for dividends. Pension funds, charities and trusts and some individuals are dependent upon income from dividends to meet their needs. In the case of trusts, this need for income could not be overcome by substituting regular scrip issues for cash dividends as the scrip would be considered as capital in the trust fund's hands not income, and this would disturb the rights of a life tenant as against the remainderman.

Other groups of shareholders, on the other hand, are more concerned with capital growth than with income. The shareholder paying the maximum rate of 98 per cent in taxation finds that dividends have little worth to him. Such shareholders have a preference for increasing the share price through retaining more earnings, or for a regular scrip issue rather than a cash dividend. Shareholders' needs would be best served if companies were able to offer a choice of either a cash dividend or a scrip issue in lieu. While this is permitted, for example, in the United States, it has not been legal in this country since April 1975.

TABLE 6.1

Effect of full and nil distributions on different groups of shareholders
(Income tax rate assumed to be 35%)

	Shareholder paying	
	'nil' tax	tax at 98%
	£	£
A. Full distribution		
Earnings available to shareholders	100	100
Corporation tax at 52%	52	52
Profit after tax	48	48
Dividend	48	48
Retained earnings	—	—
Received by shareholder:		
Dividend	48	48
Plus: Tax credit repaid	26	—
Less: Higher band tax rates and investment income surcharge	—	47
Total	74	1
B. Nil distribution		
Earnings available	100	100
Corporation tax at 52%	52	52
Profit after tax	48	48
Dividend	—	—
Retained earnings	48	48
Received by shareholder	nil	nil

The tax implications of a full distribution of earnings and a nil distribution for different groups of shareholder are shown in Table 6.1. If all earnings are distributed as dividends the institution or person who pays no tax would receive an aggregate of £74, made up of the £48 dividend and £26 tax credit which would be repaid. If no dividends are paid, however, such a shareholder would only have a claim of £48 on the additional retained earnings. The preference of this group of shareholders for dividends is therefore quite clear.

The shareholder who pays income tax at the top rate of 98 per cent on investment income would receive only £1 if all earnings are distributed, whereas if no dividends are paid he would have a claim of £48 on the retained earnings in the same way as would the non-taxpayer. If the fact of retaining an additional £48 of earnings works through to an equivalent increase in the share price, i.e., the market value of the whole equity increases by £48, this is much more valuable. If that increased value is realized by selling some shares the gain is only taxed at the capital gains tax rate of 30 per cent maximum, or the realization of the gain could be postponed well into the future.

The greatest overall value to the shareholders and the maximum market capitalization of the company's shares could be achieved if the shareholder was able to select the form of his return from the company. Since this is no longer possible the only way in which values could be maximized through dividend policy would be for some companies to follow dividend policies suited to non-taxpayers, and other companies' policies suited to the high tax-rate shareholder. Since institutions hold a high proportion of most quoted companies' ordinary share capital this is not, perhaps, a practical course of action and could produce bitter conflicts. This was illustrated in 1975 when Coats Patons proposed to omit its final dividend for the previous year to conserve cash flow by not having to pay either the dividend or the related ACT. The vociferous protests of the institutional shareholders makes it unlikely that other companies would follow the same course. Many private shareholders would have been happy with the position and in view of the common image of the private shareholder wanting to drain the last penny from a company it is interesting to note that it was the institutions who were doing all the squealing.

In considering dividend policy and the shareholders' interests directors will feel obliged to balance the interests of the different groups of shareholders unless there is a clear indication that the composition of its shareholders is heavily biased to one particular group, in which case it could pursue a dividend policy tailored to the requirements of that group. Where the board decide to pursue a policy slanted to the needs of one group it is suggested that the dividend policy the company will follow, i.e., 'maximum distribution', 'minimum dividend required to maintain trustee status', etc., should be made known so that past and future shareholders are aware of that policy.

Harmonizing company and shareholder needs

Dividend policy is frequently seen as a compromise between the competing needs of the company to retain profits to finance new investment and the needs of the shareholder for dividends. This is true in only a very limited sense. One must consider wider implications when establishing a long-term dividend policy.

There are two factors relating to dividend policy which must be fully considered, both of which concern their impact on share price. The first of these factors is the consistency of dividends. Shareholders will tend to value more highly a stream of dividends which increases regularly rather than total dividends of the same amount which show an irregular pattern with major increases and decreases, and this will be reflected in the share price. The other factor is the effect that changes in the proportion of earnings that are paid out as dividends (the dividend payout ratio) can have upon the share price.

Directors should as a matter of prudence try to smooth the pattern of dividends even if the underlying earnings from which the dividend is paid fluctuate considerably from year to year. Unless they do so, investors who are dependent upon income from shareholdings will tend not to invest in the company and this will have the effect of lowering the share price. Dividend policy in such a situation should be considered on a long-term basis in the light of the likely future range of earnings in bad years as well as good. Once this minimum/maximum level of earnings has been established the earnings trend over the next few years can be used as the basis for the year-by-year declaration of dividends, rather than using only the year's earnings.

Dividend payout ratio and the price/earnings ratio

There is much evidence both from the work of researchers and from empirical evidence that the P/E ratio is affected to a greater or lesser degree by changes in the payout ratio. The evidence is that the higher the dividend payout ratio the higher will tend to be the P/E ratio, i.e., the share price will move upwards.

The importance of the share price consideration is that it may remove the apparent competition for funds as between the ploughing back of profits into the company and paying profits out as dividends. Through its effect of increasing the share price, the use of funds to pay the higher dividend may make available to the company additional external funds which more than outweigh the cost of paying that extra dividend. Consider the illustration in Table 6.2. The company illustrated has one million ordinary shares issued and

TABLE 6.2
Effect of different payout ratios on the share price

Payout ratio %	Price/earnings ratio	Cost of dividend £	Share price p	Market capitalization £
60	15	60 000	150	1·5 million
30	10	30 000	100	1 million

earns 10p per ordinary share. If the company pays out 60 per cent of its earnings as a dividend (6p per share) the market would value the shares on the basis of a P/E of, say, 15, thus giving a share price of 150p and a market capitalization for the whole of the ordinary share capital of £1·5 million.

If, however, the company only pays out 30 per cent of its earnings as dividends the market capitalizes the shares on the basis of a P/E of, say, only 10, giving a share price of 100p and a market capitalization of the equity of only £1 million.

The payment of a 6p dividend which costs only £30 000 more than the cost of a 3p dividend would effectively increase the market capitalization of the company by some £500 000. The significance of this is apparent where the company wishes to make a take-over bid for another company on the basis of an exchange of shares for a purchase consideration of £250 000. If it is following a payout ratio of 30 per cent it would have to issue 250 000 of its own shares to acquire the company. On the other hand, if it is following the 60 per cent payout pattern then it would only have to offer 166 667 of its own shares to acquire the other company. The higher payout ratio would also assist in the raising of new share capital. Not only does the higher share price make the company a more attractive proposition from the investor's point of view but it can also reduce the dilution effect of issuing new shares. For example, if the company wished to raise £300 000 by means of a rights issue to shareholders at 40 per cent below the current market price, then if the company had followed the 30 per cent payout ratio it would have to offer 500 000 new shares to its shareholders, i.e., a rights issue of 1 for 2 at an offer price of 60p. If it had followed the 60 per cent payout ratio it would only have had to offer 333 333 new shares, i.e., a rights issue of 1 for 3 at an issue price of 90p. If the company is to raise capital by issuing new shares to people who are not already shareholders or to shareholders in proportions different to those on which shares are already held, this would become a matter of concern not only for the company but also for the individual shareholders.

The directors need to know whether or not changing the payout ratio for their own company would in fact have an effect on the share price. A study carried out by the author of the companies comprising three industry groups in the FT Actuaries Index over a 10-year period suggests that there is a wide disparity between companies, even within the same industry, as to the effects of movements in the payout ratio. In some cases there is an almost perfect correlation between movements in the payout ratio and movements in the P/E ratio. An illustration of such a correlation is that shown in Fig. 6.1 for International Timber. If the past record of a company showed a similar correlation the directors could make their dividend policy decision on the basis of a reasonable certainty that they could influence share price through moving the payout ratio.

Other companies had a much less positive correlation than that shown for International Timber, but nevertheless the dividend payout ratio was exercising some effect on the share price. The only way for directors to take account of these relationships in their dividend policy decision is to examine the historical relationship between the payout ratio and the P/E for their

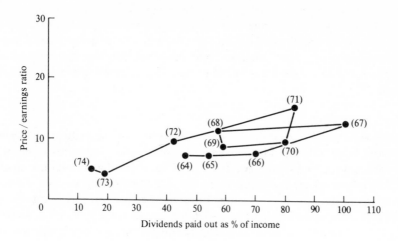

FIG. 6.1
Correlation between payout and price/earnings ratios: International Timber 1964–74

company over a period of years to establish what degree of correlation there is between the two.

Capital structure

The shareholders' interests and the long-term viability of the company are both affected to a considerable extent by the manner in which the directors decide to finance the long-term capital requirements of the company. The issue hinges on what proportion of the company's capital employed is financed by long-term debt and other fixed return securities.

The decision on the capital structure should be based upon:
1. The 'gearing' effect on earnings per share.
2. The increased exposure to risk of business failure as the proportion of long-term debt increases.
3. The way that control of the company may be affected.

The following analysis is only concerned with the basic financial management aspects of the decision. Other shorter-term factors may also have to be taken into account. For example, in times of rapid inflation, borrowing money puts some of the burden of inflation onto other people. If the rate of inflation is 25 per cent per year then if the company can borrow money at, say, 16 per cent on which tax relief is obtained, thus reducing the cost to about 8 per cent, then the company is paying a negative rate of interest for using that money of about 17 per cent. The tax system may also make dividend payments more expensive for a company than the equivalent amount of interest cost. In the UK, for example, in 1975 interest is tax relieved at a tax rate of 52 per cent so the net cost is only 48 per cent of the gross interest paid. Dividends, on the other hand, are paid out of income that has suffered tax at the rate of 52 per cent, but only a 35 per cent tax credit goes with the dividend.

The gearing effect on EPS

In the right conditions the higher the proportion of the company's capital employed that is financed by debt and other fixed return funds, the higher will be the earnings per share. The right conditions are that the return on the capital employed for the company as a whole must be higher than the cost of servicing the debt and providing other fixed returns. If this primary condition is not met then gearing can operate to depress the earnings per share.

The gearing effect can be illustrated by comparing two companies with the same capital employed and the same underlying level of profitability as shown in Table 6.3. Company A has a capital employed of £1000 all of which is

TABLE 6.3
The gearing effect

	Company A £		Company B £
Ordinary shareholders' funds	1000	10% Loan Ordinary shareholders' funds	500 500
Operating profit	150		—— 1000
Return on capital employed (ROCE)	15%	Operating profit *Less*: Interest	—— 150 50
		Profit available to shareholders	—— 100 ══
Return on equity (ROE)	15%	Return on capital employed (ROCE) Return on equity (ROE)	15% 20%

financed by ordinary shareholders' funds. It has an operating profit, i.e., before interest and tax, of £150 per year. The ROCE and ROE are both the same at 15 per cent. Company B has the same capital employed of £1000 and the same operating profit. In this case, however, half of the capital employed has been financed by a 10 per cent loan and only the balance by ordinary shareholders' funds. While the ROCE is the same as for Company A, the ROE has increased to 20 per cent. This increase is due to the fact that the cost of the loan is only 10 per cent (ignoring taxation), but when that money is put to work in the company it is able to earn 15 per cent—the difference between the two rates adding directly to the profit attributable to the ordinary shareholder.

The problem that directors are most likely to meet in practice is the need to raise additional capital by an established company. A critical factor in that decision is the impact that using different sources of capital would have on the earnings per share. The use of debt in that financing decision would have the effect of altering the ratio between debt and equity and increase the gearing effect. It is true that short-term considerations would have to be taken into account at each financing decision. For example, the state of the capital markets may influence a particular choice. In the long term, however, the directors have a duty to decide what is the most appropriate capital structure for their company and ensure that the balance between debt and equity which results from that decision is broadly adhered to over time.

Since the future level of earnings cannot be known with certainty at the time the financing decision is taken, the effects of the different financing choices should be explored over a range of possible areas and preferably displayed in the form of a graph. Let us take as an example the case of a company which has issued one million £1 ordinary shares. Its current earnings before interest and taxation (operating profit) is £250 000 and it pays a dividend of 5p per share. The board of directors are considering raising new capital of £500 000 and two methods of doing so are being considered. Method A is to make a rights issue of 1 for 2 at par. Method B is to issue a new 10 per cent debenture for £500 000 (costs of the issue are ignored). The earnings per share at the present time can be computed as follows:

		£000s
Earnings before interest and tax (EBIT)		250
Interest		nil
Earnings before tax		250
Tax at, say, 50%		125
Earnings after tax		125
Number of shares issued		1 million
Earnings per share (EPS)	$\dfrac{£125\,000}{1\ \text{million}} =$	12·5p

If the capital structures that would ensue from using financial methods A and B outlined above are now used to compute the earnings per share for the present rate of earnings we will have three values for EPS which relate to three different capital structures and which are comparable since they are all based upon the same EBIT.

The calculation of the EPS values is shown below.

	Existing capital structure	Capital structure financing method A	financing method B
		£000s	
Earnings before interest and tax (EBIT)	250	250	250
Interest	—	—	50
Earnings before tax	250	250	200
Tax at 50%	125	125	100
Earnings after tax available to shareholders	125	125	100
Number of shares issued	1·0 million	1·5 million	1·0 million
Earnings per share (EPS)	12·5p	8·33p	10·0p

If EPS values based on a different level of earnings are now calculated these together with those already calculated provide two points of reference for graphing the curves which represent the way EPS changes for different levels of earnings for each of the capital structures. Assume for the second calculation earnings before interest and tax are £500 000. This would produce the values below.

	Existing capital structure	Capital structure financing method A	financing method B
		£000s	
Earnings before interest and tax (EBIT)	500	500	500
Interest	—	—	50
Earnings before tax	500	500	450
Tax at 50%	250	250	225
Earnings after tax available to shareholders	250	250	225
Number of shares issued	1·0 million	1·5 million	1·0 million
Earnings per share (EPS)	25p	16·66p	22·5p

From the two calculations that have been carried out it can be seen that the EPS under the existing capital structure would increase from 12·5p per share when EBIT is £250 000 to 25p per share when EBIT is £500 000. Similar

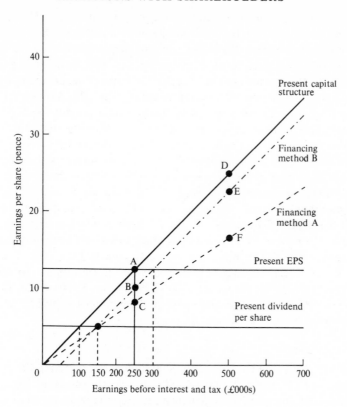

FIG. 6.2
EPS for different levels of earnings

values for the two capital structures that would emerge from the financing operation are also shown. These values provide the basis for showing how the EPS values would change over any range of EBIT required, as shown in Fig. 6.2.

The range of earnings is shown on the horizontal axis. £700 000 has been used as the maximum on the scale but this could be extended to any required value. At £250 000 EBIT the EPS values for the three capital structures are shown at A, B, and C. At the £500 000 value the EPS are shown in a similar manner. The two points for each of the capital structures are now joined and show a curve from which can be read off the EPS value for any level of earnings for each of the capital structures.

The curves for both the existing capital structure and financing method A cut the intersection of the two axes since in neither case is there any prior charge for interest or preference dividends against profit. The curve for financing method B cuts the horizontal axis at a point which represents the EBIT required to service the interest cost of the debenture, i.e., at £50 000.

Figure 6.2 shows that there is a breakeven point between financing methods A and B. If EBIT are lower than £150 000 the rights issue method of financing the new capital requirement would give the highest EPS. Above that level of earnings the debenture method of financing would provide the higher EPS. If future earnings are likely to exceed that level then the debenture method would be the most advantageous to the shareholders in EPS terms.

The financing chart shows other factors that the directors should consider before making their choice between the two financing methods. As far as the present dividend cover is concerned the 5p dividend is covered if earnings are higher than £100 000. The same rate of dividend would require earnings of at least £150 000 to cover its cost if either of the financing methods is adopted. The present EPS of 12·5p per share could only be maintained under financing method B if earnings rise to at least £300 000 from the present level of £250 000. The maintenance of the EPS is not appropriate to the rights issue alternative as the shares are normally offered at a price below the ruling market price. The special requirements of maintaining a given EPS level when a rights issue is made are discussed later.

Risk

The benefits that could accrue to the shareholders by adopting the debenture issue method of raising the new capital are clearly shown in Fig. 6.2 providing that earnings are expected to increase from the present level of £250 000. The adding of long-term debt to a company's capital structure, however, has another effect which the directors cannot ignore—it increases the risk of business failure. The servicing of interest and loan repayments imposes a burden on the company's cash flow and in periods of recession the cash flows might not be able to support that burden and the company is forced into default on its debt.

The excessive use of debt also reduces the company's flexibility in future financing choices. If the company's maximum debt potential has been absorbed by current financing operations then the board may well have only the option of going to shareholders for new funds when the occasion next arises. If that need arises during a period where, because of stock market or other conditions, it is impossible to raise new equity the company is then left with no alternative source of funds to fall back on. The objective of the directors' financing policy should be to optimize the amount of debt to be used in the capital structure, taking into account the gearing effect on shareholders' earnings, the additions to risk, and the reduction in the flexibility of future financing choices.

Traditionally, acceptable debt levels in the capital structure have been determined by multiples of interest and asset cover, e.g., interest should be covered, say, four times by earnings, or the loan should be covered, say, twice by assets. Such criteria are used by the lenders of money to try to ensure that they are adequately covered against loss if the company meets difficulties. The board should determine what is an acceptable level from the company's point of view rather than that of people lending money to it. This can only be accomplished by a review of the likely pattern of cash flows over the life of the loan.

The critical point for a company's cash flows is when it meets a period of recession. During such a period losses may be incurred but the negative cash flow aspect of such losses is obscured by the release of cash through the running down of stocks and debtors, and perhaps the suspension of new capital investment. The real problem emerges when the company begins to pull out of the recession and cash is needed once more to invest in increased stocks and debtors. Then the drain of cash during the recession begins to show and there may be two or three years of major negative or minimal cash flows which would not be able to support large-scale debt service. How and to what extent this situation can arise varies from company to company and can only be resolved through the preparation of year-by-year cash flows for the company based upon the extent of any possible recession that may be encountered.

Such recessional cash flow forecasts can only be made with the cooperation of the board. Management does not sit idly by when the company moves into recession—it responds to that situation with appropriate measures. The board should decide now what those measures will be, so that the preparation of the cash flow forecasts can be made on the basis of essential contingency planning. Responses to recession include:

—Possible reductions in prices to maintain volume, with consequential effects on margins.

—Reduction of fixed costs.

—Use of more extended credit in the marketing strategy.

—Cutting investment in fixed assets.

—Cutting dividends.

—Considering whether or not to retain skilled staff through the recession, even though there is insufficient work.

One of the difficulties of management's response to recession is that frequently it is not immediately apparent that one is in a period of recession. The initial downturn of business is seen as a temporary affair. Some of the responses outlined above may not therefore be implemented until the company is well into the recession.

The role of the board in such contingency planning cannot be emphasized too much, not only for its implication for the financing strategy, but also as a major contribution to policy development.[1]

[1] For illustration of the detailed recession planning see M. G. Wright *Financial Management*, chapter 14 (McGraw-Hill, 1970).

Control

Where new shares are to be issued on other than a rights basis the implications for the control of the company should not be ignored. Even if there is a rights issue, when controlling shareholders do not have the funds available to take up their rights the same result can ensue from the operation. Any situation where the company's shares are closely held requires some consideration of the effect of the issue of new shares upon the position of the major share-holders.

Rights issues

A rights issue is the offer of sale of new shares to the existing shareholders so that each can purchase new shares in proportion to his existing holding. Thus, if all the new shares are taken up by the shareholders concerned the percentage of the company's share capital held by each shareholder would be the same after the issue as it was before the issue. The rights issue is effected by sending to shareholders a renounceable letter of allotment for the appropriate number of shares. The shareholder then has three courses of action open to him. He can:

1. Accept the allotment of shares and pay the subscription money.
2. Sell the renounceable letter of allotment to someone else who does want to acquire the company's shares.
3. Do nothing.

There is normally a market for the 'rights' in the same way as there is for the company's shares during the period of the rights issue. The price at which the rights are traded depends upon the relationship between the subscription price for the rights and the market price for the old shares 'ex rights'. The higher this difference, the greater is the value of the right. The potential investor in the company has two methods of acquiring a shareholding in the company. He can buy the old shares 'ex rights' or he can buy the right to buy the new shares at the subscription price for the issue. Because of arbitrage the two avenues present roughly the same total cost of buying the shares. The major difference is that the sale of rights is free of stamp duty for the period while the letter of allotment is renounceable.

The third option above becomes more difficult the lower the subscription price for the new shares in relation to the old share price. If there is a large difference the old shares will have a much lower market price after the issue is completed. The shareholder must therefore sell the rights in the market and compensate himself for that loss, or take up the rights. He could steer a middle course by selling enough rights to pay for the acquisition price for the new shares. What he cannot do is to sit tight and do nothing or he will lose some of the value of his shares.

If the new shares are to be issued at a price near to the current market price, the directors may feel constrained to arrange for the issue to be underwritten so that any shares not taken up by shareholders are taken up by the underwriters. This, however, costs money, perhaps some $2\frac{1}{2}$ per cent of the value of the issue, and could be avoided by offering more shares at a lower price since the relative position of shareholders to each other is unaffected by the number of shares issued. Where this is the case it may also be possible to ensure 100 per cent acceptance by allowing the shareholders to apply for any rights not taken up by other shareholders.

The greatest confusion with rights issues is the assumption that there is a conflict between the interests of the shareholder and that of the company. One frequently reads press comment along the lines that Company X is forced to concede better terms for a rights issue. This is nonsense. The interests of the company and the shareholder are identical. There is a common problem —to raise the required funds for the company with the least cost. The number of shares issued to achieve that purpose is irrelevant since each shareholder who takes up his rights has exactly the same percentage of the issued capital as he had before the issue.

The great pity is that in the process of trying to squeeze what they think is the maximum value for a rights issue the board pays unnecessary underwriting commission and all too many issues fail because the issue price is pitched too close to the market price which, as a consequence, falls below the issue price so that there is no incentive whatsoever to shareholders to take up the rights. In time of dividend limitation a rights issue at well below the market price is also a useful way of increasing the return to the shareholder.

More fundamental than the question of the price for a new issue is for the board to ensure that when they call for a rights issue the new funds will generate a large enough increase in earnings to maintain the shareholders' overall values. If this is not done the shareholder can lose very heavily. Take the company illustrated in Fig. 6.2. The present EPS is 12·5p per share. If investors rate the company's shares on the basis of a P/E of 20 the share price would be 250p per share. Taking financing method A, for every two shares already held the shareholder is now invited to subscribe for one new share at a price of £1.00. The position of a shareholder holding two shares would then be as follows:

Value of existing holding, $2 \times 250p$	$= 500p$
Rights issue, $1 \times 100p$	$= 100$
Required value of holding after the issue, $3 \times 200p$	$600p$

If the P/E of 20 is maintained after the issue then a price of 200p per share after the issue would require EPS of 10p. Since the company would then have 1·5 million shares issued this would mean that the after-tax profits available to the shareholders must rise to 1·5 million × 10p or £150 000. The earnings before tax required to achieve this would be £300 000. Unless the directors can see earnings before tax rising to this level as a result of the issue then that issue should be abandoned. If it is proceeded with, the shareholders will lose on two counts. First, the EPS will fall below the 10p required to maintain the share price and, second, because of the fall in the EPS it is likely that the market will revise downwards the appropriate P/E ratio. Let us assume, for example, that earnings only rise from £250 000 to £280 000. The after-tax earnings would only be £140 000 and with 1·5 million shares issued this would provide an EPS of 9·33p instead of the expected 10p. If the P/E remains at 20 this would give a share price of 186·6p. If, however, the market in addition reduced its P/E rating to 17 because of the falling EPS, this would reduce the share price to 9.33p × 17 = 158.6p. For the three shares then held this gives a total market value of 475·8p, an amount which is less than the market value of the two shares the shareholder owned before he was asked to put into the company an extra 100p.

It is this two-way squeeze which is the great danger where there is a rights issue. Damage done to the share price and investor confidence through such a situation may take many years to repair and make the possibility of raising money in the future through the rights issue medium that much more difficult.

7.
Interpreting financial results

The data exhibited in the financial report present merely a stewardship report. If the information is to have real meaning both for management and the users of the report it must be subjected to a process of analysis and interpretation. This process is founded on the comparison of related data in the accounts. For example, the value of the profit for the period stated in £s does not have very much meaning. To say that X Ltd had a profit last year of £10 000 tells one very little about that company's performance—it might be a small company with less than £100 000 of capital employed or it might be a major international company. If, however, the profit is related to the resources that have had to be employed to earn that profit one does have an index of performance.

The same analytical tools that are developed for interpreting the annual report can also be extended to interpret and help control operations on a much shorter time scale, say a month. Such ratios can play an important role in the overall control of the business. The director should therefore consider what he needs to know about his company and its operations, how much of that information can be derived from the annual financial report and more frequent management reports, and how people outside the business will use the same techniques for their own purposes.

What the director needs to know about his company
The principal matters on which the director requires information are outlined below.

How efficient have he and his fellow directors been in putting the resources of the company to work? The measurement of the directors' overall effectiveness is the profit earned in relation to the resources used. One must look not only at the overall level of profitability that this expresses but also all those aspects of operations which help to determine the level of profitability.

The economic trade-offs between operating factors Operating factors do not stand on their own but are related to other operating factors. For example, it is desirable to reduce the investment in stocks to as low a figure as is possible to effect a more efficient use of capital. If that process is taken too far a 'stock-out' position may arise with the consequential loss of sales and gross profit. Stock policy should be based upon optimizing the balance between these two aspects of stockholding.

The effect the financing decision has upon the shareholder The combination of sources of funds used to finance the business can have an important impact upon the return to the shareholders and upon risk and control. Analysis of the financial report can reveal the impact that the financing decisions have had upon shareholders.

The ongoing viability of the company The company must be in a sound financial position, able to meet its day-to-day commitments to outside persons. Trends in the balance sheet can indicate where this position is deteriorating or improving and highlight those factors which are causing the change.

The relative efficiency of operating areas Where it is possible to obtain meaningful comparisons with similar companies, or with similar operating units within the same company, an assessment may be made of the relative efficiency of different operational aspects of the company.

How the outside world views the company Values placed upon the company by its shareholders and potential investors can be examined and related to the company's activities and its future needs for new capital.

Trends and causes for all of these areas should be known to the directors and those factors which cause changes in the various relationships should be the subject of detailed study in the planning and control process. Unless directors are fully informed and institute the appropriate controls they cannot be in effective control of their company.

What are ratios?

Ratio analysis is concerned with expressing relationships between inputs and and outputs (for example, in relating the capital employed and the profit that results from its employment, or the sales achieved per square foot of display space), with relationships between different aspects of the business which are crucial for its continuing existence (such as that between short-term liabilities and short-term assets reflecting the ability of the company to meet its obligations to creditors), and with attitudes such as those expressed by the share price on the stock exchange compared with earnings per share.

The objective of ratio analysis should, therefore, be to construct a framework of such relationships which are important for the success of the individual company. One part of this framework brings together all those aspects of the business which contribute to *profitability* both for the company and its shareholders. Another part of the framework assesses the *liquidity* of the company. The remaining part reflects the company's standing in the outside world. Included in those aspects which contribute to profitability are those operating relationships which are peculiar to the individual industry or firm.

How to use ratios

From the director's point of view the principal use of ratios should be to detect trends within his own company. Adverse trends in ratios should be the trigger which sets off a more detailed investigation into the problem. In a sense they are a problem-identification tool rather thon a problem-solving tool. This is why they should form part of the overall reporting system. To some extent they may sometimes indicate areas for further exploration. For example, if profitability has declined they may indicate whether it is the margin on sales or less effective use of assets which is the culprit.

Limitations to the use of ratios

There are some limitations to the effective use of ratios. This is particularly so where one wants to make a comparison between different companies. The difficulties arise from three factors.

1. Valuation differences: the policies adopted by the companies for the valuation of assets may be different. This particularly applies to whether or not the fixed asset values have been adjusted to present-day values. Fortunately such differences are lessened as inflation accounting is introduced.
2. Accounting policy differences: the policies adopted by the companies for such matters as depreciation, recovery of research and development expenditure, etc., will affect the comparisons.
3. Operational differences: the way the different companies operate and the segment of the industry they occupy can affect comparisons between them. For example, one company might own its property but another rent it; one company might produce and sell its own branded products while another is a sub-contractor to such a company.

In order to make meaningful comparisons between companies it is essential that the differences in 1 and 2 above should be fully compensated for and that comparisons are only made with companies which have similar operating characteristics. Any comparison made without such adjustment should be treated with extreme caution.

Inflation is also a factor which can invalidate comparisons because of its effect on the money measure of the assets of the company and its effect on the measurement of profit. As methods of accounting for inflation are introduced they should eliminate differences arising from this cause and will make it easier to compare one company with another.

Interfirm comparisons

Where it is possible to make comparisons with other companies some form of interfirm comparison can be a meaningful aid to management, when used in the appropriate circumstances. In order to be fully effective, the companies' accounts should be adjusted to eliminate the differences highlighted above, so that the results are stated on a common, comparable basis. In this situation the detailed operating ratios appropriate for the type of activity can be compared with those of other companies so as to highlight operating areas where performance differs. Again, ratios are used to isolate problem areas, not to find the solutions. Interfirm comparison groups are usually formed under the aegis of such bodies as trade associations. Perhaps the best-known organization is the Centre for Interfirm Comparison which is managed by the British Institute of Management.

Profitability ratios

The principal ratio that measures profitability is the *return on capital employed* (ROCE). This is a ratio which measures output to resource use—in this case, profit earned to the capital required to earn that profit. Once this has been ascertained the next steps are to explore the factors which have determined what that level of profitability should be. This requires a step-by-step analysis of factors which determine profitability.

Return on capital employed

This ratio measures the profit before or after tax, but before charging interest on long-term loans, as a percentage of the capital employed. It is taken before charging long-term interest because it is not concerned with *how* the capital employed has been raised but merely with, given the capital available from whatever source, how successful the board has been in earning a return on that capital. All the illustrations of ratios in this chapter are from Incognito Ltd as shown in Tables 7.1 and 7.2. It is important to define clearly the terms used in this ratio.

Capital employed It is now generally accepted that capital employed can be defined as the total of all the *long-term funds* employed, i.e., all shareholders' funds, plus long-term borrowing, plus any deferred items, such as deferred tax. Alternatively, it can be defined as the *net assets* of the company, i.e., fixed and current assets less current liabilities. Because of the balance sheet equality the two values are the same. For Incognito the value for the first year is £2 760 000.

Profit Whether profit is measured before or after tax depends upon the purpose for which the analysis is being undertaken. If it is to be an appraisal of internal operating performance it may be preferable to use profit before tax. If it is for the use of an investor who wishes to appraise the company as an entity then after-tax profit might be more appropriate. Whichever level is selected it should be made clear which is being used.

TABLE 7.1
Incognito Ltd: Balance sheets for three years

	19×1		19×2		19×3	
			£000s			
Uses of funds						
Fixed assets (net)		2043		2374		3362
Current assets:						
Stocks and work in progress	615		1136		1203	
Debtors	642		908		1050	
Cash	155		614		130	
	—— 1412		—— 2658		—— 2383	
		3455		5032		5745
Less:						
Current liabilities:						
Creditors	150		172		435	
Taxation	295		310		390	
Dividends	120		160		140	
Bank overdraft	130		—		371	
	—— 695		—— 642		—— 1336	
Net assets		2760		4390		4409
Financed by						
Shareholders' funds:						
Issued share capital £1 ordinary shares		1000		1000		1000
Capital reserves		850		797		865
Retained profits		600		703		735
		2450		2500		2600
10% Debenture 19ʸ9		—		1500		1500
Deferred taxation		310		390		309
		2760		4390		4409

The reason for using profit before charging interest on long-term borrowing can be demonstrated by the data in Table 6.3 on p. 70. Both of the companies shown have £1000 of capital available and on that capital management has been able to earn an operating profit of £150. It is right to say that they are equally successful in putting the funds of their respective companies to work. It is only when considering the interests of the ordinary shareholders that the cost of prior charges, such as interest, must be taken into account. (If bank borrowing is used consistently year by year it may be treated as long-term borrowing in this analysis.) Using the data for Incognito Ltd the ROCE for the three years is as follows (using the after-tax value):

$$19 \times 1 \qquad\qquad 19 \times 2 \qquad\qquad 19 \times 3$$
$$(1)\ ROCE\ \frac{312 \times 100}{2760} = 11{\cdot}30\% \quad \frac{472 \times 100}{4390} = 10{\cdot}75\% \quad \frac{383 \times 100}{4409} = 8{\cdot}69\%$$

The profit of £472 used in year 19×2 is made up of the after-tax profit for

TABLE 7.2
Incognito Ltd: Profit and loss accounts for three years

	19×1		19×2		19×3	
			£000s			
Sales	3900	100·0	4730	100·0	5280	100·0
Cost of goods sold	2600	66·7	3050	64·5	3731	70·7
Gross profit	1300	33·3	1680	35·5	1549	29·3
Operating expenses	678	17·4	743	15·7	782	14·8
Operating profit	622	15·9	937	19·8	767	14·5
Interest	—	—	150	3·2	150	2·8
Profit before tax	622	15·9	787	16·6	617	11·7
Taxation at 50%	310		390		309	
Profit after tax	312		397		308	
Ordinary dividends	200	(20p per share)	294	(29·4p per share)	276	(27·6p per share)
Retained profits for the year	112		103		32	
Earnings per share	31·2p		39·7p		30·8p	
Share price at end of year	290p		480p		210p	

the year of £397 000 to which has been added the after-tax cost of the interest which amounts to £75 000.

From the ratios at (1) it can be seen that there has been a decline in profitability in 19×2 and 19×3. It can also be seen that a much higher *profit* was earned in 19×2 than 19×1 but, because an even higher volume of resources has had to be used to earn that profit, *profitability* is lower. What was the cause of the decline in profitability over the two years? It is in the search for such answers that lies the key to the effective use of ratios. In order to explore this two further ratios must be computed—the *margin on sales* and the *turnover of capital employed*.

Margin on sales

This is the familiar concept of profit in relationship to the sales or value of work done. The measure of profit used for this ratio should be the same as that used for ROCE. The profit is then simply expressed as a percentage of the sales value. For Incognito Ltd the ratios for the three years are:

	19×1	*19×2*	*19×3*
(2) *Margin on sales*	$\dfrac{312 \times 100}{3900} = 8\cdot0\%$	$\dfrac{472 \times 100}{4730} = 9\cdot98\%$	$\dfrac{383 \times 100}{5280} = 7\cdot25\%$

Turnover of capital employed

The function of this ratio is to express how effectively management is controlling the use of resources. One of the definitions of capital employed is that of net assets, therefore this ratio is concerned with whether management is making the best use of the funds locked up in each type of asset in relation to the level of sales and making the best use of short-term credit. The latter factor is, however, conditioned by liquidity constraints and the way suppliers might retaliate if too extensive use is made of trade credit. Management's attention is therefore devoted to the level of investment in assets in relation to the volume of work or sales. The ratios for Incognito Ltd are:

$$\begin{array}{cccc} & 19\times1 & 19\times2 & 19\times3 \\ (3)\ \textit{Turnover of} & \dfrac{3900}{2760} = 1\cdot41\ \text{times} & \dfrac{4730}{4390} = 1\cdot08 & \dfrac{5280}{4409} = 1\cdot20 \\ \textit{capital employed} \end{array}$$

As can be seen, the ratio is calculated by dividing the sales for the year by the capital employed at the end of the year.

What determines profitability?

The two factors which determine profitability can now be defined. The two ratios (2) and (3) when multiplied together give the ROCE. Mathematically this must be so since the three ratios have been based upon only three values—sales, profit, and capital employed. It has a major significance for management. Profitability as defined by ROCE is determined by only two factors—those of margin on sales and efficiency in turnover of capital employed. Overall profitability can only be improved by improving one or other of the two ratios.

The relationship between these three ratios forms the first stage of the build-up of the financial framework of the company. The ROCE in Fig. 7.1

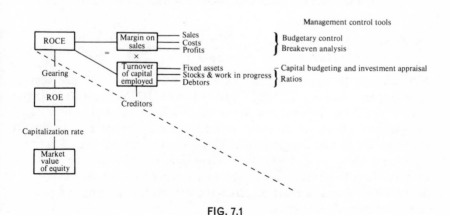

FIG. 7.1
The financial framework

is first of all analysed in terms of profit margin and turnover of capital employed. These must then be explored in turn to investigate what factors determine each. The determinants of the margin on sales are the volume of sales and the amount of the various groups of costs incurred in running the business. Analysis here must be concentrated upon isolating and relating to sales value all the elements of cost, such as direct materials, labour costs, etc. From the management control point of view, attention should be paid to planning and controlling the levels of sales and costs with the objective of controlling the profit margin. This is the function of the budgetary control system. The factors which determine the turnover of capital employed are principally the amounts that the company invests in fixed assets, stock and work in progress, and debtors in relation to the volume of sales. Because of the long-term nature of investment in fixed assets there must be some form of capital budgeting and investment appraisal before the investment is made. The capital budget is required to evaluate the overall spending on fixed investment because of the potential implications of this for liquidity, and the appraisal system to ensure that the investment will have a beneficial effect on ROCE. Once the funds have been committed to such a use, management can no longer control the level of investment but merely record whether the decision was a wise one or not. Investments in stocks and work in progress are short-term uses of funds and ratios can be used to help to control these.

Return on equity

This ratio examines profitability from the point of view of the investor and answers the question 'What is the rate of return on the ordinary shareholders' funds?' It is based upon two values—the value of the profits which are attributable to the ordinary shareholders and the value of their funds employed in the business. This latter value includes not only the issued capital but also the undistributed gains and profits. For Incognito Ltd the ratios are:

$$\begin{array}{cccc} & 19\times1 & 19\times2 & 19\times3 \\ (4) \; \textit{Return on} & \dfrac{312\times100}{2450} = 12\cdot73\% & \dfrac{397\times100}{2500} = 15\cdot88\% & \dfrac{308\times100}{2600} = 11\cdot85\% \\ \textit{equity} & & & \end{array}$$

Note that in the year 19×2 the ROE has risen from 12·73 per cent to 15·88 per cent, whereas the ROCE declined from 11·30 per cent to 10·75 per cent. Why did this happen? It is due to the fact that the company introduced gearing into the capital structure. In that year it borrowed £1·5 million in the form of a 10 per cent debenture. This costs the company only 5 per cent after tax, while it earned a ROCE of over 10 per cent after tax. The difference between these two rates has accrued to the benefit of the ordinary shareholders. This shows in practical terms the benefits that gearing can provide to the ordinary shareholders.

This element can now be added to the financial framework shown in Fig.

7.1. The ROCE modified by the gearing introduced into the capital structure provides the ROE. This can then be taken one step further. If the earnings attributable to the ordinary shareholders are multiplied by a capitalization rate, e.g., the multiple applied to earnings when deciding the price one is prepared to pay for the company or for its shares, then one arrives at the market value of the equity—a value which the directors should be trying to maximize in the long term.

If a diagonal line is drawn across the financial framework one can distinguish the two principal functions of financial management. Above the diagonal one is looking inwards into the company at its operating activities to ascertain what contributes to the return on capital employed—in other words, how management is using the funds that are available. Below the diagonal one is looking outwards from the company to explore its relationships with the financial markets. For example, the capitalization rate is not determined by the company but by investors.

Turnover of stock

This measures the number of times stocks and work in progress are turned over in each year and is computed by dividing the stock value at the end of the year into the cost of sales for the year, or if that value is not known, the sales value. The ratios for Incognito Ltd are:

	19 × 1	*19 × 2*	*19 × 3*
(5) *Turnover of stock*	$\dfrac{2600}{615} = 4\cdot22$ times	$\dfrac{3050}{1136} = 2\cdot68$ times	$\dfrac{3731}{1203} = 3\cdot10$ times

When used for internal control a more precise measure is required as a year's cost of sales would not be an adequate basis. Depending upon the manufacturing time cycle for the company's products, the cost of sales for the last one or two months would be used instead of the year's value. In addition separate ratios would be calculated for material stocks, work in progress, and finished stocks, with possible separate calculations for different product groups.

Debtors

The two factors which determine the level of funds locked up in debtors are the value of sales and the time taken to collect amounts owing. For example, if the company has credit sales of £100 000 per month and takes on average three months to collect amounts owing then debtors will stand at £300 000 in its balance sheet. The method of expressing the debtors ratio is usually that it represents so many days' sales. This provides an index against sales and can also be compared with the official credit period.

The calculation of the ratio is made in two stages. First the average sales per calendar day must be computed (calendar days since the company's credit terms are in calendar days). Once the average sales per calendar day has been computed the result is divided into the debtors at the end of the period. Thus for Incognito Ltd the ratio for the year 19×1 is computed as follows:

$$\text{Average daily sales:} \quad \frac{3900}{365} = 10.68$$

$$\begin{array}{l} \text{Number of days' sales} \\ \text{outstanding as debtors:} \end{array} \quad \frac{642}{10.68} = 60 \text{ days}$$

The ratios for the three years are:

	19×1	19×2	19×3
(6) *Debtors ratio*	60 days	70 days	73 days

For internal control purposes the average day's sales would be based upon the credit sales of the last one or two months only. Movements month by month during the current year would be compared with similar movements during the previous year to allow for seasonal variations in the ratio.

The above are the principal profitability ratios which are applicable to all types of business. They can be backed up by more detailed ratios which reflect operating relationships peculiar to individual industries.

Liquidity ratios

The function of the liquidity ratios is to test the ability of the company to meet its ongoing commitments to third parties and is founded upon the relationship between the short- and long-term assets and liabilities.

Current ratio

The principal liquidity ratio is the current ratio. As its name implies it measures the relationship between the current assets and current liabilities. For Incognito Ltd the three ratios are:

	19×1	19×2	19×3
(7) *Current ratio*	$\dfrac{1412}{695} = 2.03:1$	$\dfrac{2658}{642} = 4.14:1$	$\dfrac{2383}{1336} = 1.78:1$

As expressed, the ratio is simply saying that in 19×1 current assets covered current liabilities 2.03 times. The conventional norm for this ratio is 2:1 although there are industry variations due to different practices within those industries.

The directors' principal interest in this ratio should be the factors which determine the ratio. These are discussed in some length in chapter 9. It is sufficient at this stage to say that, although the ratio is measured by the relationship between current assets and liabilities, it is determined by the relationship between long-term assets and long-term funds. There must be sufficient long-term funds to cover long-term assets with enough left over to cover the necessary margin between current assets and current liabilities to provide the required ratio.

Quick or acid test ratio

Current assets include a major asset which might not be very liquid—that is to say, stocks and work in progress. These may be in the form of material stocks and work in progress, so that manufacturing has to be completed before the goods could be sold. The quick ratio omits this asset from the computation, otherwise the ratio is computed in the same way as the current ratio. The three ratios for Incognito Ltd are:

$$19 \times 1 \qquad\qquad 19 \times 2 \qquad\qquad 19 \times 3$$

$$(8) \; Quick \; ratio \quad \frac{797}{695} = 1 \cdot 15 : 1 \quad \frac{1522}{642} = 2 \cdot 37 : 1 \quad \frac{1180}{1336} = 0 \cdot 88 : 1$$

The norm for this ratio is 1:1

Financing ratio

The proportion of long-term debt in the capital structure influences the long-term stability of the company. The greater the proportion of the capital employed financed by long-term debt the greater the risk to the company of failure. There are a number of ways this relationship can be expressed, e.g., debt/equity, debt/capital employed. For illustrative purposes the latter method is used. For Incognito Ltd the three years' ratios are:

$$19 \times 1 \qquad\qquad 19 \times 2 \qquad\qquad 19 \times 3$$

$$(9) \; Debt/capital \quad \text{NIL} \quad \frac{1500 \times 100}{4390} = 34\% \quad \frac{1500 \times 100}{4409} = 34\%$$
$$employed$$

Investor's ratios

The directors must also be aware of the ratios that may be used by investors in appraising the company as an investment.

Earnings per share

Companies now publish the earnings per share as provided for in SSAP 3. For Incognito Ltd the three years' EPS values are shown below and have been calculated by dividing the earnings in each year attributable to the ordinary shareholders by the number of ordinary shares issued:

$$19 \times 1 \qquad\qquad 19 \times 2 \qquad\qquad 19 \times 3$$

$$(10) \; EPS \quad \frac{312}{1000} = 31 \cdot 2p \quad \frac{397}{1000} = 39 \cdot 7p \quad \frac{308}{1000} = 30 \cdot 8p$$

Price/earnings ratio

The price/earnings ratio is ascertained by dividing the current market price of the company's shares by the EPS. The P/E ratio will be constantly changing during the year as the market price of the shares changes. Its significance to investors is not the absolute value of the P/E but how it compares with the P/E of similar companies. If it is higher than similar companies it means that investors expect the company's earnings to rise at a faster rate than other companies, and vice versa.

The P/E for Incognito Ltd for the three years based upon the year-end share price is:

$$
\begin{array}{cccc}
& 19\times 1 & 19\times 2 & 19\times 3 \\
(11)\ \textit{Price/earnings} & \dfrac{290}{31\cdot 2}=9\cdot 3 & \dfrac{480}{39\cdot 7}=12\cdot 1 & \dfrac{210}{30\cdot 8}=6\cdot 8 \\
\textit{ratio} & & &
\end{array}
$$

Times cover for the dividend

This ratio expresses the number of times the available earnings cover the cost of the dividend. If the company has any preference shares all the earnings after tax are available for dividend cover. When all prior charges, such as preference dividends, have been deducted then the remaining earnings are all available to cover the cost of the ordinary dividend. The cover for the dividends for the three years for Incognito Ltd is as follows:

$$
\begin{array}{cccc}
& 19\times 1 & 19\times 2 & 19\times 3 \\
(12)\ \textit{Times cover} & \dfrac{312}{200}=1\cdot 56\ \text{times} & \dfrac{397}{294}=1\cdot 35\ \text{times} & \dfrac{308}{276}=1\cdot 12\ \text{times}
\end{array}
$$

Dividend yield

This ratio expresses the gross return an investor would receive if he invests in the company at the present market price of the shares, i.e., it is the gross amount of dividend received for each £100 invested at current share prices. The gross amount is the dividend per share plus the related tax credit and is therefore comparable with before-tax yields from other investments. For Incognito Ltd the values for the three years are:

$$
\begin{array}{cccc}
& 19\times 1 & 19\times 2 & 19\times 3 \\
(13)\ \textit{Gross yield} & 9\cdot 85\% & 8\cdot 75\% & 18\cdot 78\% \\
\textit{(at }30\%\textit{ tax rate)} & & &
\end{array}
$$

The yield for the year 19×1 is calculated as follows:

Dividend per share 20p

Tax credit $\frac{3}{7}$ 8·57p

28·57

$$\text{Yield} \quad \frac{28\cdot57 \times 100}{290} \quad = \quad 9\cdot85\%$$

Operating ratios

The ratios discussed so far have a common application to almost any type of business, although the ratios may differ in value from one type of business to another. When one looks at the more detailed factors that determine the margin on sales and the turnover of capital employed there may be very large industry and even intra-industry variations. The use of detailed operating ratios depends, therefore, upon management identifying the ratios which represent important operational relationships for that particular business and making arrangements for these to be reported upon at frequent intervals.

Businesses are so diverse that it is impossible in a book of this nature to itemize what ratios could be used. A detailed exposition of such ratios is given by C. A. Westwick in his book *How to Use Management Ratios* (Gower Press, 1972). Examples that demonstrate the wide range of ratios include sales per square foot of display space, marketing costs to quotations made or sales orders received, buying costs to purchases, power to actual output, man days lost to man days worked, etc. The interrelationships between the ratios that are appropriate for the company can then be built up into a pyramid leading to ROCE.

8.

Planning for growth

Directors should give very careful consideration to their role in determining the long-term growth pattern of their company. It is a function which is particularly the province of the board since it is the medium through which the directors express their leadership of the organization and stamp on the company the imprint of its future development. The whole character and ethos of the company is vitally affected by the decisions taken in determining the future pattern of growth, and the planning processes used should be designed to bring together the different interests which exist in any organization and direct them towards the achievement of common goals. It may sometimes be questioned whether, given the many uncertainties which exist in the economic, political and social environments, planning can effectively contribute to the success of a business. One can only deplore the uncertainties, many of which are imposed by politicians. Every extra uncertainty makes the decision process that much harder. Nevertheless, any activity can only be run successfully if a clear plan of action is drawn up and the responses to as many contingencies as possible determined in advance.

Consider, for example, someone proposing to lead an expedition to the South Pole. This is an activity surrounded by many uncertainties and hazards, and the only chance of a successful outcome to the expedition is for careful, meticulous planning down to the last detail. This planning would include such aspects as:

—Clearly defining the objective of the expedition, e.g., scientific objective, personal prestige, etc.
—Studying the climatic and geographical conditions of the area.
—Planning the route.
—Planning the siting of base and advanced camps.
—Deciding the timing of each part of the activity.
—Deciding what human skills are required in the light of the objective of the expedition and how it is proposed to achieve it.
—Deciding what physical resources are required, such as vehicles, stores, etc.
—Setting up contingency plans in case things go wrong.
—Planning how to raise the funds that will be needed to finance the activities decided on above.

To embark on an expedition without such planning is to court disaster and the same applies to the business world—unless the leaders of a company carry out similar planning the business has much less chance of success.

Unforeseen events are almost certain to occur which tend to throw the company off its intended course. The best way of dealing with these is to identify as far as possible what those events might be and to include in the long-term plans the appropriate contingency plans for dealing with them if they do in fact occur. All too often the unexpected comes like a bolt out of the blue and leads to panic reactions by managers. In such a situation inappropriate decisions may be taken which damage the company's long-term interests. Such damage can be minimized if the possibility of such a happening is identified and the response of management to that happening determined in advance.

It is essential that the directors become committed to and involved in long-term planning for growth. While in a large organization the preparation of forecasts, determining the economic climate, etc., may be delegated to staff assigned for that purpose, the decisions on which the eventual plans are based must be those of the directors—they cannot be delegated without the directors abdicating their role. The key role played by long-term planning is illustrated by the fact that planning in any other area of the business is determined by the goals and policies adopted. For example, the decision processes for any area start with the decisions made in the long-term plans relating to that area, e.g., capital investment (the general pattern of new investment must conform with the requirements of the long-term plan) or management development (this will be determined by the skills required as shown in the plans). In other words, the short-term decisions that are made in running the company cannot be made without full reference to the requirements of the long-term plans and the objectives of the company.

The purpose of planning for growth

Just as someone planning to lead an expedition to the South Pole would have a purpose in doing so, so the directors should be quite clear what the company should try to achieve in the long term. Before planning proper can take place it is necessary to establish a set of common goals or objectives for the company to achieve over the planning period. Unless what the company is trying to achieve is set out clearly, with no ambiguities, the consequent planning is likely to be woolly.

Once the company's objectives have been defined the planning process can start. The planning process itself is concerned with *how* the company is to organize itself so that it can achieve those objectives. It consists of devising an overall strategy for the company to follow and the various functional strategies and policies that must be adopted. It is these which set the framework for consequent short-term decisions in those areas.

What goals are adopted varies from company to company but, as is suggested later, all companies share a common goal—that is to make a profit—and the other goals are in the last resort judged by the way that they affect profit. The final decision on what the goals are to be rests with the directors. They must bear the full responsibility for the outcome of the plans adopted to meet those goals. Where detailed planning is delegated the directors must set the guidelines within which the staff involved must work.

Planning should be from the top down, not the bottom up

It follows from the directors' primary responsibility for long-term planning that the plans should be formulated at the highest level in the business, first of all in terms of what is to be achieved by the company as a whole, and within that framework what must be contributed by each of the lower echelons of management. This can be contrasted with the alternative method of planning (or perhaps non-planning) which is to allow decisions about the long-term future of the company to be made at line-manager level, with the board trying to coordinate the various plans that are put before it. The latter method is unlikely to produce the cohesive plan that is so essential if the company is to be successful.

Conglomerates and very large companies where there is a high level of devolution of decision making often appear to transgress this rule, but this is only superficially the case. The basic financial objectives are still set by the board of the main company and it is that board which allocates the available resources to the operating groups. Through this process the main board retains control and direction of the overall balance within the group. Within the constraint of resources the boards of the operating companies then proceed to carry out long-term planning in very much the same way as if they were independent companies, although the ultimate approval of their plans lies with the board of directors of the main company.

Unity of purpose

Any business which is trying to achieve conflicting objectives simultaneously is unlikely to be successful. One of the functions of long-term planning should be to ensure that the objectives and policies being pursued by management at all levels are fully coordinated and designed to provide the maximum probability that the company as a whole will be successful in achieving its corporate goals.

This cannot be so if managers are unaware of what the company is trying to achieve and the part that they are required to play. Communication of the corporate objectives and the policies the board wish to pursue should be made as far down the managerial hierarchy as possible and each manager made aware of how his personal contribution fits in to the overall requirement.

Reconciling personal and corporate objectives

It is by no means true that managers below the board level perceive the objectives of their area of activity in the same way as the board. Each individual has a range of personal objectives which can at times positively create conflicts within the organization. This is particularly true in the case of the larger organizations which tend to be divided into semi-autonomous entities, each with its own management. In this situation there may exist quite deep conflicts between what each manager sees as being necessary for his operational area and what is required from that operational area in order to meet the corporate goals. For example, the manager of a product-based division where the division's product is on the declining part of the product life cycle may see his personal objectives as being best served by a continuing high level of investment of resources in that product in order to prolong its profitability for as long as is possible. This is a not unnatural situation since the role and standing of the manager in the company and to some extent in society is linked with the product, and he may see his employment security as being closely related to the continuing viability of that product.

From the point of view of the requirements of the company's long-term goals, however, it may be more desirable to stop further investment in that product and to begin moving resources away from it to support new products which are at the beginning of their life cycle. The directors should ensure that the long-term planning procedures adopted are such that potential conflicts can be identified and through a process of discussion with the managers involved reconciled with each other. Simply to force through the corporate plan without ensuring that each manager is fully committed to it is likely to reduce the possibility of fully meeting the corporate objectives.

Setting the pattern for short-term planning

All too often short-term planning is carried out simply by looking at the present and previous years' activities, and, after making what are thought to be suitable adjustments, projecting the past pattern of activities into the future and using this as the base for the short-term plans. Through such planning methods the directors would effectively allow short-term events to determine the long-term future of the company. It is rather like the driver of a car trying to drive with the windscreen painted over. He can see what is behind and on either side but not what is in front of him. He is likely to meet a sudden end. And without the forward view provided by long-term planning the company may meet a sudden end as it encounters unforeseen adverse conditions.

Short-term planning should start with an appraisal of what needs to be done next year to move forward towards the long-term goals. In the light of that appraisal and of any short-term influences which must be allowed for next year, a plan of action can be prepared which should move the company in the desired direction. Ongoing policies such as management and organizational development must also be tailored to meet the long-term requirements.

Duties of the directors

The primary requirement is that the directors should have a wholehearted commitment to the effective use of long-term planning. Unless they have this commitment any system devised is unlikely to be effective since staff will feel, probably correctly, that when faced with a major decision, the directors will make it on an *ad hoc* basis without reference to the long-term plans. Planning in such a framework simply becomes shadow boxing—a formality which has to be gone through because the procedures are laid down but which has little practical effect on the way in which the business is run. If, on the other hand, it is seen that the directors not only play a part in setting the long-term plans, but also ensure that decision taking occurs within the framework of reference set by those plans, the commitment of other people further down the managerial hierarchy will be that much greater. One is not suggesting that the long-term plans should be rigid and that anything which does not conform with them should be rejected—rather that, if a major policy decision should indicate a course of action contrary to the long-term plan, then the plan itself should be reappraised. One can then see whether or not the course of action would conflict with the revised plan.

In addition to their commitment to long-term planning as a management tool, the directors have a duty to ensure that the right procedures for the planning process are set up, taking into account the particular needs of the organizational structure. This framework should ensure the following.

1. There is an adequate system for monitoring and forecasting environmental and other changes. A prerequisite for good long-term planning is full information of the likely trends in social, technological, and other changes which may affect the company in the future. This information is required not only so that the necessary adjustments can be made to the company's future pattern of activities, but also to identify possible market opportunities which such changes may present to the company. Information is also required on the activity of competitors and some forecast should be made of their likely future behaviour, particularly in such matters as new product development and the installation of major new production units. Much of the information for the preparation of forecasts can be derived from an analysis of published material. In some cases, however, it may be necessary to commission specific investigations to obtain the information.

2. The commercial opportunities of internal activities must be identified. In a large organization, people's horizons tend to be restricted to the rather narrow sphere within which they work. Events which do not immediately impinge on that sphere are likely to be ignored and this could well be to the detriment of the company. Penicillin is a classic case of the failure to

realize the true importance of a discovery. Fleming actually discovered the effect of penicillin in 1928, but because it happened when he was doing research on bacterial diseases he thought little about it and did nothing more than to publish a paper on it. It was only at the beginning of the Second World War that two medical students searching for more effective treatment of war wounds came upon the report and found out exactly what penicillin would do.

It is essential that the organizational framework should be such as to maximize the probability of the commercial possibilities of discoveries being recognized and acted upon. This is particularly true in the case of research and development activities. The scientific mind does not readily relate the scientific experiment with its commercial significance, with the result that a useful contribution to the company's future prosperity may be lost. There should be the maximum amount of liaison between the research teams and marketing and production management so that both the research and operating sides of the business are fully aware of what is happening in the other's sphere of activity and are able to appreciate more fully their particular problems and requirements.

3. There should be a formal organization for dealing with long-term planning centrally and at manager responsibility level. In the large company the formal organization for long-term planning is likely to consist of a specialized central planning group working directly under the control of the board, and able to call upon the services of similar planning groups at divisional or other levels. The planning groups would be of a size to include the range of specialist skills required, such as economists, sociologists, scientists, etc., as well as representatives of the financial function.

In a small company it may not be feasible to employ specialist staff and the functions must be carried out as additional duties by existing staff. The internal skills may have to be supplemented by the *ad hoc* use of outside consultants.

Whatever the formal structure of the long-term planning activity, there is one essential factor that should be understood by directors and others and one where the directors can largely influence attitudes—that is that the decisions on which the plans are based must be those of managers and directors and not those of the planning staff. A system which is seen by employees as being the creature of the planning group, or accountants, or any other interest group in the company, is unlikely to achieve the wholehearted acceptance by managers that is required. The role of planning staff and any other groups involved in the planning process is that of providing and interpreting the data on which directors and managers should base their decisions, and subsequently helping to formulate those decisions in detailed value and other terms. They should not on any account usurp the decision function itself.

4. There should be a periodic review of the plans. Long-term plans, once drawn up, are not immutable for the whole of the planning period but should be reviewed to meet changing circumstances. The directors should ensure that factors which may require a revision of the plans are recognized and reported upon so that a revision can be initiated. One such factor would be where a major investment project is submitted which does not fit in with the long-term plans. Either the plans must be revised to accommodate the investment project or the project must be discarded.

The planning period

Because of the wide diversity of business activities undertaken by companies it is impossible to set a common time scale for long-term planning. The time scale chosen should be based upon the length of time that major product or service development takes to implement in that particular business. In the aerospace or nuclear energy industries, for example, that period may be a very long one, possibly 20–25 years or more. In other fields of activity it may be quite short, e.g., the production and merchandizing in the fashion industry, where change is very rapid. The time scale set for the planning period may also have to take into account the time it requires to effect major structural changes within the company, such as changes in the technologies employed in the production process.

Stages in the planning process

Once they have decided upon the most appropriate planning period the directors' functions are to:
1. Define the corporate objectives, i.e., what the company is expected to achieve over the planning period.
2. Decide on the means to be used to reach those objectives, i.e., the corporate strategy.
3. State what is required from each section of the company as part of the fulfilment of that strategy.
4. Set up some method of monitoring progress towards the achievement of the corporate objectives.

Corporate objectives

The directors should be quite clear as to what is meant by corporate objectives. Confusion is often created because the means by which the objectives are to be achieved are stated as objectives, as are statements of the company's attitudes towards ethical matters. Consider, for example, the following statement of corporate objectives:
1. To provide an adequate return to investors in the company.
2. To set up the most advanced technologies in production techniques.

3. To ensure a happy, satisfied workforce.

4. To increase the market share of the company's products to 40 per cent.

5. To support industry training and development schemes.

Statement 1 is a statement of what the company wants to achieve and is properly stated as an objective. Statements 3 and 5, on the other hand, are statements about *how* the company intends to behave towards other groups of people. Statements 2 and 4 are statements about *how* the company intends to set about achieving the objective defined in statement 1.

Profit as the primary objective

There is a clear implication in the previous paragraph that, as a last resort, statements 2 and 4 would be tested against the return to investor or some other profitability criterion and if they had an adverse effect on that criterion such statements would be amended. This brings us to consider the *primus inter pares* standing of the objective in statement 1. Many writers today would accept that profit is the primary objective, since if a company is to stay in business in the private sector it must achieve a level of profit which would enable it to attract funds from investors to finance growth. Even the concept of survival put forward by some writers as the primary objective must in the last resort depend upon earning sufficient profits to sustain the continued existence of the company.

The real test is, of course, to ask what would happen if an objective is proposed that would conflict with the requirements of the profit objective by leading to low profitability or actual losses. Such an objective would surely be reviewed and amended until the required level of profitability could be achieved. All proposed objectives must in the last resort be tested against this central requirement of profitability .

This does not mean to say that profits must be maximized at all costs, but merely that a certain minimum level of profitability must be achieved if the company is to be able to continue to attract the new capital that it requires. Directors may be forgiven for believing that in the present social climate their primary duties should be to the employees, customers, or the community at large. The truth of the matter is that the company can only continue to serve the interests of employees, customers, etc., if it remains a profitable viable organization. If it fails in this duty then, as stated in chapter 6, the employment it provides, the contribution its products or services makes to the community will be lost, as will its contribution to the tax revenue of the country.

What level of profit?

Accepting that profit is the primary objective directors must determine what is the minimum level of profit that the board should accept as a target over the planning period. Bearing in mind that the company can only grow if it can attract new funds, i.e., that investors perceive the company as an attractive investment medium, this minimum acceptable level of profit must be one that will provide an overall return to investors in terms of income and capital growth which compares favourably with the returns investors can earn on other investments, whether in companies or other investment mediums, such as government stocks, after allowing for differences in risk.

Lord Stokes criticized 'the City' for valuing some office blocks in London at a figure higher than the market capitalization for British Leyland which contributed so much to the UK's exports. Yet events proved that the investors' judgements were correct. British Leyland did not turn out to be an attractive investment and pension fund and insurance company fund managers and the private investors preferred to place their funds where they could earn a more adequate return. Investors are not philanthropists and many, such as pension fund managers and trustees, have a positive duty to earn the maximum return consistent with security on the funds that they manage.

British Leyland is also a good illustration of the identity of interests between share holders and employees in the long term. Had it not been for government intervention, the failure of British Leyland to earn adequate profits would have put the employment of over 100 000 people at risk. That employment is supported by the enforced investment of taxpayers' funds. Whether that will prove to be a wise decision may not be known for some years. However, the same support cannot be given indiscriminately by governments: in other less spectacular failures no such support would be forthcoming and jobs would be lost.

In the process of determining the minimum level of profit required the directors must decide upon the long-term strategy for financing the company and in particular the balance between long-term debt and equity. The implications of using debt to finance the company have been discussed in the previous chapter. The decision on the long-term balance between different sources of funds is necessary so that the profit required to cover the interest costs of debt can be determined. The board's decision on dividend policy then enables an estimate to be made of the dividend return to shareholders and the likely basis on which the market would value the shares. Thus some conclusions can be drawn as to the likely overall return to shareholders over the planning period.

Because of the inter-relationships shown in the financial framework on p. 85, the level of profit required to provide an adequate return to shareholders can be related to the capital employed to show the ROCE that must be earned. This follows once the balance between debt and equity and interest rates have been determined. Then, given the dividend policy, the cost of dividends to the company and the amount of earnings that could be retained year by year can be computed.

Determining the strategy

It is not proposed to go in depth into the details of strategy formulation but merely to outline the process. Instead, the financial tests for any given strategy and how these can be devised and measured will be dealt with in detail.

Determining the profit gap

Most products and services have a fairly well-defined life cycle, at least in their present form and through present methods of distribution. Initially there is a period of development and the market launch; the product then begins to gain customer acceptance and eventually reaches a period of maximum profitability. Some time after that a general decline in its profitability sets in because customers' needs change or new products are developed, or competitors devise more effective merchandizing techniques. The point is eventually reached where the product or service is no longer viable.

The time covered by the life cycle varies considerably. In some cases a few years only, in others it may appear to last almost indefinitely, as with basic foods. But even in the latter case methods of production and serving the customer (such as convenience foods) will require the present pattern to change in some way.

It follows from this that if no changes are made in the company's services or products the level of profit from its existing activities is likely sooner or later to decline. The first step in determining the 'profit gap' is to take the company as it is presently constituted and forecast the level of profits that would be earned if no changes are made to products or the way in which the company operates. This level of profit may rise for some years but eventually will begin to fall.

The difference between the forecast level of profits from the existing business and the level that is required to give an adequate return to shareholders is the profit gap. This gap shows the minimum additional profit that must be earned by one means or another if the company is to remain viable. The function of strategy formulation is to determine the means that are to be adopted by the company to close that gap.

The strategy

Devising a strategy for a company is a crucial test of managerial skills and entrepreneurial judgement. Those skills and judgement can only be exercised effectively if the directors and managers involved in the process are fully informed of the likely trends in the social and economic environments over the planning period and the direction of technological change. There must also be an in-depth appraisal of the company itself with a view to determining the strengths and weaknesses of the organization, its products, skills, resources, management structure, and so on, and what has caused it to be successful or not successful in the past.

The strategy should be based upon identifying opportunities which the changing environment may present and which the skills, etc., of the company would enable it to exploit most effectively. As the policies are explored and possible strategies hammered out, a plan for meeting the profit gap will gradually be formed. As potential strategies emerge, they must be tested against the profit requirement and from those that meet that requirement a selection must be made. It is not an easy task and will probably have to be tested and revised a number of times before an acceptable plan emerges.

When the strategy has been formalized it will set the framework for such matters as:
—Research and development.
—Product or service range.
—Marketing strategy.
—Production strategy, e.g., production techniques, quality standards, etc.
—Financial strategy.
—Physical resources required.
—Human skills required.
—Organizational development.

The profit criterion

As the possible strategies emerge, the profit and cash flow patterns that would ensue from them should be measured to ascertain whether or not the projected profit pattern would provide the necessary rate of return to investors and whether the requirement for new funds can be met and from what sources. This process of measurement can be illustrated using the following data.

Planner Ltd has at the present time a capital employed of £1·24 million and is able to earn a profit before tax of £250 000. It has no long-term debt. The share capital comprises 600 000 £1 ordinary shares on which a dividend of 10p per share is paid. The directors are examining a 10-year planning period and have made the following provisional decisions regarding future growth:

1. Capital employed should expand at the rate of 20 per cent compound per year.
2. ROCE should average 20 per cent pre-tax.
3. Use will be made of long-term debt. Immediate capital needs will be met from this source, but debt should not exceed approximately one third of total capital employed.
4. Approximately 50 per cent of attributable earnings will be paid out by way of ordinary dividends.
5. It is expected that if the financial objectives are achieved the present P/E ratio of 10 will rise to 15 by the end of the 10-year period.
6. Interest rates are expected to be 10 per cent.
7. Tax is expected to be at the rate of 50 per cent.

8. Growth will be by internal development rather than by external acquisition. (This illustration assumes no inflation. The special problems that arise in times of inflation are dealt with elsewhere.)

A financial plan that meets the requirements set out above is shown in Table 8.1. Section A shows the planned growth in the capital employed, the earnings before and after tax for each of the years, the interest cost of planned long-term debt, and dividends and retentions. Section B shows how the additional capital requirements are to be met and the planned composition of long-term funds in each of the years. Section C shows the number of ordinary shares that would be issued, the investment ratios, and the projected share price.

The additional capital required over and above retentions in the first three years is shown as being financed by long-term loans as provided for in 3 above. At the end of that period debt would represent approximately 29 per cent of total capital employed. The table shows debt being added to in each of those three years. In practice it might be desirable to make only one issue of debentures, or other form of loan stock, during the three-year period at a time when the best rates can be obtained. In this case any short-term need would be met by bank borrowing and any surplus funds lent out short term to earn a return.

In the fourth year it is likely that any new capital required would be financed by a rights issue since to add to long-term debt in that year would take the percentage of debt to capital employed above the one-third that the directors have laid down. The funding operations in each of the remaining years is designed to maintain the debt ratio at about the one-third level.

The shareholders' position is shown in section C. The share price assumptions are based upon the assumptions that P/E will move from 10 to 15 over the 10-year period. The directors would have to consider whether the cash demands on shareholders in the form of rights issues in the last five years would be excessive. If they feel that this would be the case consideration would have to be given to the possibility of increasing the debt/capital employed ratio during that period. Otherwise consideration should be given to restricting the growth rate in those years to one that would have a lower demand on the shareholders.

Further consideration can be given to the overall position of the shareholders by examining the effect of the plan on a representative shareholding, assuming that the company meets its targets (see Table 8.2). Assume that the shareholder starts the period owning 200 shares having a market value of £400. He takes up the rights issues included in the plan and at the end of the period would own 800 shares which would have a market value of £3112. If sold on the last day of the planning period for that value the shareholder would incur capital gains tax of £593 (realized £3112 less cost £1135 equals a gain of £1977 at 30 per cent tax). Taking into account the dividends

TABLE 8.1
Financial plan for Planner Ltd[1]

Section A

	Present	Year 1	2	3	4	5	6	7	8	9	10
Capital employed	1240	1449	1728	2077	2489	2994	3585	4302	5162	6194	7425
Profit before interest and tax	250	288	346	415	498	597	717	860	1032	1239	1487
Interest	—	14	34	60	60	98	98	152	152	152	244
Profit before tax	250	274	312	355	438	499	619	708	880	1087	1243
Corporation tax	125	137	156	177	219	249	309	354	440	543	621
After-tax profit available to the shareholders	125	137	156	178	219	250	310	354	440	544	622
Dividends	60	68	78	89	109	125	155	177	220	272	311
Retained profits	65	69	78	89	110	125	155	177	220	272	311

Section B

	Year 1	2	3	4	5	6	7	8	9	10
Source of new capital:										
Retained profits	69	78	89	110	125	155	177	220	272	311
Long-term debt	140	200	260	—	380	—	540	—	—	920
Rights issues	—	—	—	302	—	436	—	640	760	—
	209	278	349	412	505	591	717	860	1032	1231

[1] Figures quoted in this table are for £000s.

	Year 1	2	3	4	5	6	7	8	9	10
Composition of capital employed:										
Long-term debt	140	340	600	600	980	980	1520	1520	1520	2440
Shareholders' funds	1309	1388	1477	1889	2014	2605	2782	3642	4674	4985
	1449	1728	2077	2489	2994	3585	4302	5162	6194	7425
Percentage debt to capital employed	10	20	29	24	33	27	35	29	25	33

Section C

	Year 1	2	3	4	5	6	7	8	9	10
Number of shares issued at end of year	600	600	600	900	900	1200	1200	1800	2400	2400
Earnings per share	22·8p	26·0p	29·7p	24·3p	27·8p	25·8p	29·5p	24·4p	22·7p	25·9p
Price/earnings ratio	10·5	11·0	11·5	12·0	12·5	13·0	13·5	14·0	14·5	15·0
Dividend per share	11·3p	13·0p	14·8p	12·1p	13·9p	12·9p	14·75p	12·2p	11·3p	13·0p
Projected share price at end of each year	239p	286p	342p	292p	347p	335p	398p	342p	329p	389p
Rights issue terms	—	—	—	1 for 2 at 105p (less expenses of issue)	—	1 for 3 at 150p (less expenses of issue)	—	1 for 2 at 110p (less expenses of issues)	1 for 3 at 130p	—

TABLE 8.2
Effect of Planner Ltd's long-term plans on the individual shareholder

Year	Number of shares owned	Cost of shares £	Dividends received £	Amount realized on sale of shares	Cash flow £	PV factor for 19%	Present value £
0	200	400	—	—	(400)	1·000	(400)
1	200	—	23	—	23	0·840	19·3
2	200	—	26	—	26	0·706	18·4
8	200	—	30	—	30	0·583	17·5
4	300	105	36	—	(69)	0·499	(34·4)
5	300	—	42	—	42	0·419	17·6
6	400	150	52	—	(98)	0·352	(34·5)
7	400	—	59	—	59	0·296	17·5
8	600	220	73	—	(147)	0·249	(36·6)
9	800	260	90	—	(170)	0·209	(35·5)
10	800	—	104	2519	2623	0·176	461·6
							10·9

received during the period the total overall return on the investment would be 19 per cent after tax. This is a higher return than the market as a whole offers and would make the company an attractive investment and ensure its ability to attract the funds that it would require to finance its growth over the 10-year period.

9.

Financial planning for survival

The events of the mid-1970s in the UK brought home to many boards of directors the fact that earning a profit is not enough to secure the survival of the company. Company after company, including some of the largest in the country, found that other people were no longer willing to subscribe new capital to support their operations, either in the form of new loans or new share capital. Some found that the only way to survive as an entity was to turn to the government for aid. While this move was successful in some cases it was not in others, and even where it was successful the original shareholders found that they had lost control of the company and perhaps the whole of their interest in it.

In order to survive the various crises which may arise during its life, the financial structure of the company must be kept in balance. It is keeping the right balance at all times that is the key to survival, just as a boxer's survival in a fight depends upon keeping his balance. If the company is caught off its financial balance then, like the boxer, it may go down.

The directors must also consider the question of investor confidence in the company which will, of course, be largely determined by its financial stability. Seemingly strong companies can be put at risk where there is a crisis of confidence in its future. Its creditors try to limit their risk by restricting trade credit extended to the company or allowing none at all. Financial institutions who have loaned money short term may refuse further lending and gradually a financial chasm opens up in front of the company. The maintenance of a strong financial base in order to secure creditor and investor confidence should form a major plank in the directors' overall plans for the company. Risk taking is, of course, a proper function of management, but risk should only be accepted in the financial structure planning after the full effects of the financing plan on creditor and investor confidence have been assessed. Once risk in the financing of the business is seen as being at an unacceptable level the crisis in confidence can quickly snowball, feeding on its own fears and bringing the company to its knees.

For some years I have umpired a business game centred on the building and construction industry which requires competing teams to bid for contracts and manage them. At the same time each team has only limited financial resources. Time and time again companies have bid for and gained contracts way beyond the capacity of their financial resources, without any consultation with their banker umpires to see whether finance will be available. It is a situation which one suspects is continuously repeated in real life. Overtrading is a factor which regularly contributes to or directly causes the downfall of companies.

The plain truth is that no concern can carry on a level of business which its capital base is unable to support. Sooner or later it is likely to meet a situation where its dangerous financial position is unmasked. The capital base of long-term funds must be secured before the level of trading increases to such an extent that the company's future is put at risk. To accede to a rapidly expanding level of trading before having secured this financial base is to put the whole business at risk and is a negation of a director's responsibilities. Nemesis has an unfortunate habit of catching up with companies where this balance between resources and activities is not maintained. Yet it is a lesson that is continually having to be relearned. Both sales managers and bank loan officers can wear rose-tinted spectacles and lead a company on a wave of euphoria to a position where it is exposed to risk. Witness the sorry state of the secondary banks (and indeed the high loss provisions of the clearing banks) in the mid-1970s because of the euphoria in the property boom of a year or two earlier. At that time huge volumes of funds were locked up in financing property acquisitions or developments which turned sour when property values sagged. Depositors seeing a risk to their saving began a run of withdrawals. There would have been a spectacular chain reaction of bankruptcies leading right up to and possibly involving the major banks had not the Bank of England stepped in and together with the main banks provided support of over £1000 million.

What causes business failure

The risks involved in the financing decisions can best be illustrated by looking at the combination of circumstances which can bring about the liquidation of a company. It is usually the combination of three states at the same point in time which triggers the financial crisis.

1. Liquidity declines to a point where it becomes critical, forcing the directors to consider some form of financing operation.
2. The existence of an already high level of debt (often with a prior charge on assets) precludes additional borrowing.
3. The level of profitability is so low that investors would not be prepared to invest more money in the firm at that time.

These three factors occurring at the same time present a strong possibility that the company will be forced into liquidation, and even if it is not there will be a long period of retrenchment and convalescence. Items 1 and 2 above are within the control of the directors and in planning these two aspects of the company's finance they should take into account the possibility of their leading to the situation outlined. Item 3 is only partly within the control of the board since external factors may have a serious effect on the company's profitability. Planning for 1 and 2 should therefore take into account the possibility of recessional periods occurring.

Inflation may also jeopardize the financial structure of the company. The special considerations that must be taken into account to deal with inflation are treated separately in chapter 14.

The balance between long-term and short-term assets and liabilities

It has already been demonstrated when dealing with the analysis of liquidity that the liquidity ratios are determined by the relationship between long-term assets and liabilities, although they are measured by comparing short-term assets with short-term liabilities. The longer-term control of liquidity therefore rests upon the planning and control of long-term investment and at the same time ensuring that the planned investment in long-term assets can be financed by additional long-term funds. The raising of such funds should not be left to the last moment, but raised at the earliest favourable market opportunity.

The short-term control of liquidity within the long-term framework so established should then be based upon adequate controls of the short-term uses of funds, in particular the amount of funds absorbed by increases in the values of stocks and work in progress and debtors.

The long-term balance

The golden rule for industrial companies is that all long-term uses of funds must be financed by long-term funds and that in addition there should be a sufficient surplus of long-term funds to finance enough of the short-term uses to ensure adequate liquidity. Financial institutions, such as banks, hire-purchase companies and building societies, can breach this rule because they arrange their affairs in such a way that depositors have enough confidence that they can obtain repayment of monies deposited as and when required. This can be achieved by the institution keeping a substantial proportion of its funds in a highly liquid form, and having substantial cash flows arising from loan repayments.

The key is confidence. Once an institution loses the confidence of investors it is in danger of being unable to meet its commitments since it could not repay all depositors if they required repayment at the same time. For example, the Derby Building Society had to be rescued by fellow building societies at the time of the Rolls-Royce debacle. The society's depositors believed that the ability of borrowers to repay their loans would be affected by the local unemployment arising from the closing of Rolls-Royce, thus seriously endangering the society's cash flows and its ability to repay depositors. Once confidence is lost in such a situation the collapse of the institution is self-generating, as each new doubt about the soundness of the business creates more demands for repayment thus turning doubt into reality and adding new doubts.

The industrial company, because of its exposure to the commercial risks of the markets it operates in, is highly unlikely to inspire the confidence of depositors in such a way that use could be made of this form of short-term funds. (Attempts have been made to do so, e.g., the Davis Investment Group which collapsed in 1967.) The task of the directors, therefore, is to consider how best they can secure the appropriate balance between the long-term funds and the long-term uses of funds.

Why short-term borrowing may appear preferable to long-term borrowing

In a period of high interest rates directors may consider it unwise to commit the company to paying such high rates over long periods of time, and therefore only to borrow for short periods. There is the hope that when interest rates fall to more normal levels the requirements of the company can then be re-financed by long-term funds at lower rates of interest. This is a serious consideration where interest rates are, say, 15 per cent. This could impose serious burdens on a company if it borrowed at such a rate for 25 years and a year or two later interest rates fell to, say, 8 per cent.

The attraction of borrowing short in such circumstances should be considered in the light of the impact it may have on risk. The company is faced with a continuing period during which there are frequent maturities of its short-term debt. Each maturity will normally be re-financed by raising new short-term loans, but if one of these re-funding operations takes place during a period when it is difficult to raise new capital of any sort, then the company is at risk. The commitment of the company to pay high interest rates over long periods of time may impose a burden on the company but it does not expose it to the hazards of continuing maturities represented by borrowing short term.

The company that relies on bank overdrafts for financing what are essentially long-term needs must also face the possibility that the bank may call in the loan or place limits on its lending which would expose the company to the risk of not having enough funds to continue. Such action is more probable in times of severe economic difficulties which would make it awkward to replace that source of funds at that time.

Investment in long-term assets

If a company spends more of its funds on fixed assets without securing the necessary long-term funds to finance those acquisitions then the liquidity ratios will decline, and, if the spending persists, bring about a liquidity crisis. The impact of such investment is shown in the following example. Before the additional investment of £100 in fixed assets the company has a satisfactory current ratio of 2:1. That investment, however, increases the amount of the company's funds required to finance long-term investment and as a result reduces the current ratio to 1·33:1. Since no new long-term funds have been raised the additional expenditure would have to be financed by using more short-term credit, either by extending trade credit or through the use of bank overdrafts. The illustration assumes that the new fixed investment would not lead to a need for more working capital. If this were the case it would further reduce the current ratio. If the spending on fixed assets is carried on at the same level in the next year, thus bringing the ratio down to 1:1, then the company would be in a serious liquidity position.

Balance sheet before investment in new fixed assets			Balance sheet after investment in new fixed assets		
	£	£		£	£
Fixed assets		200	Fixed assets		300
Current assets	400		Current assets	400	
Less:			Less:		
Current liabilities	200		Current liabilities	300	
	——	200		——	100
Net assets		400	Net assets		400
Long-term funds		400	Long-term funds		400

If Incognito Ltd's balance sheet shown on p. 83 is referred to, it can be seen that the improvement in liquidity in the second year was due to the company raising an extra £1·5 millions by the issue of 10 per cent debentures. This more than covered the increase in the book value of fixed assets in that year of £331 000. In the third year, however, where the current ratio declined from 4·14:1 to 1·78:1 the increase in the book value of assets amounted to £988 000, whereas the addition to long-term funds in that year only amounted to £19 000 (£4 409 000 less £4 390 000).

The need for medium-term planning of long-term investment
Because of the critical role that the level of fixed investment has in determining the liquidity of a business, the amount should not be left to chance. The planning of a sound financial base must have as one of its key elements a medium-term plan of the overall capital expenditure on fixed assets. This plan should cover some three to five years' expenditure at least. It will be closely linked to the long-term plans but should take into account short-term

influences. It need not be a detailed plan but merely determine the overall limit to such expenditure.

Once that level of expenditure has been determined, the board should ensure *now* that the long-term funds are available to fund the expenditure. It is no use waiting until the expenditure makes itself felt through a reduction in the liquidity ratio. It may be too late then to do anything about raising the new capital.

The demands of working capital

Permanent demands for new capital arise from the growth in the trading activities. It is often felt that additional working capital requirements can be safely left to be financed by short-term funds, such as bank overdrafts. This is not so. If trading increases and doubles investment in such assets as stocks and debtors, then unless new fixed capital is raised to fund that increase the liquidity ratio will decline.

This is illustrated in the following example. The volume of sales and investment in current assets doubles between the two periods but there is no increase in investment in fixed assets nor in the level of long-term funds. The current ratio has declined from 2:1 to 1·33:1 because the doubled investment in current assets has had to be financed by short-term funds instead of being financed by long-term funds as it should have been. The proper way of financing the expansion would have been to introduce £200 of long-term funds so that current liabilities increase to only £400, thus maintaining the 2:1 liquidity ratio.

Balance sheet before expansion in trading			Balance sheet after expansion in trading		
	£	£		£	£
Fixed assets		200	Fixed assets		200
Current assets	400		Current assets	800	
Less:			*Less:*		
Current liabilities	200	200	Current liabilities	600	200
Net assets		400	Net assets		400
Long-term funds		400	Long-term funds		400

One cannot, of course, avoid year-by-year fluctuations in the current ratio since it is impracticable in most cases to raise new long-term loans in small amounts at a time. It would be too costly to do so. What must be watched are the longer-term trends. Between the end of the first year and the end of the third year the directors of Incognito increased the total invested in fixed assets from £2·043 millions to £3·362 millions, a rise of £1·319 millions. While the new capital raised during that period of £1·5 millions plus the additional retained profits of £135 000 were greater than that value, the excess was not enough to cover the extra working capital needs due to the expansion of trading activities. As a result, the current ratio declined from 1·6:1 to 1·57:1, in spite of the extra capital introduced.

Control of this aspect of financing must once again be based upon a consideration of the long-term plan and short-term fluctuations. The long-term plans have established in general terms the level of activity in each of the future years. The implications of those plans for working capital financing must be taken into account in determining the value of long-term capital to be financed.

Different risk characteristics of debt and shareholders' funds

Borrowing money has many attractions—in times of rapid inflation its real cost may be negative since the erosion of the capital value of the sum borrowed may be at a greater rate than the after-tax cost of the interest. The interest is fully tax relievable, whereas dividends are only partially relieved for corporation tax. Finally, as was shown in chapter 6, debt can have a considerable gearing effect on the return on shareholders' funds in the right conditions. It is therefore appropriate that the board should consider the use of long-term debt in its strategy for financing the company. It should do so, however, only after it has given full weight to the way the different sources of capital affect the financial risks.

Shareholders' funds—even those of preferential shareholders—attract no right to dividends. If, therefore, the company meets a period of unprofitable trading it has no obligation to pay anything to the shareholders—after all, they are the risk bearers.

The situation is quite different in respect of money which the company has borrowed. Here there is a debtor/creditor relationship based upon contractual rights that are legally enforceable. Rights to receive interest on the loan and repayment of the principal which are to be made on specific dates. These obligations are not dependent upon the company earning profits but are absolute requirements that the company ignores at its peril. If they are not met the people or institutions who have loaned the money will pursue their rights through the appointment of a receiver who would take over assets charged in favour of the lenders, or by petitioning the court for the winding up of the company. It is here that the real risk lies for the company—that for one reason or another its cash flow will prove to be insufficient to meet its obligations to the lenders, thus bringing about the liquidation of the company.

The balance between debt and equity

Getting the right balance between debt and equity should be examined from two points of view: how it would affect investors' attitudes towards the company, and the possibility of default by the company on its debts.

Lenders' attitudes

The attitudes of investors who might lend money to the company are conditioned by the security of any money loaned. The shareholders' funds are a cushion against loss by lenders—the higher that cushion the less likely is it that a lender will lose his money, and vice versa. Lenders are more likely to lend money if that cushion is large than if it is small. They will tend to use some yardstick related to shareholders' funds or to the net assets in determining whether to lend or not. The yardstick may be based on assets covering the sum loaned a certain number of times, or lending not exceeding a certain percentage of the shareholders' funds.

Lenders are also conscious that the values of assets shown in the balance sheet rest upon a going concern basis. The amounts that those assets would realize on a liquidation may be very much lower than the going concern valuation. Their attitudes are therefore rather conservative when it comes to determining the precise value to use as a yardstick.

Consideration is also given to whether or not the company has assets which can be pledged to the lender in some way. For example, a debenture deed provides for the assets (or specified assets) to be charged in favour of the lenders. Where a company raises a series of loans, there must be some 'pecking' order in which the loans are to be repaid if the company goes into liquidation. The debenture deed provides that the debenture holders (or a trustee acting on their behalf) have the power to appoint a receiver who takes over the assets charged and sells them, and from the proceeds of the sale the sums due to the debenture holders are repaid and any surplus handed back to the company.

When the company wants to raise additional capital its ability to do so depends upon the existence of outstanding loans and the terms upon which those loans have been raised. If assets are charged, then the company can only give inferior rights to those assets. The terms of existing borrowing may also restrict the ability of the company to increase borrowing beyond prescribed levels. In this situation the lending of further money to the company is less attractive, since others have a prior claim on the assets should the company default. The further down the pecking order for repayment the more unlikely is it that a proposed new loan would be taken up. The ability of a company to fund itself through the raising of new long-term loans is therefore affected by the volume of existing long-term debt and the extent to which its assets have been charged to others.

Borrowing up to this limit of lender acceptance reduces the flexibility of the company's future funding activities. Should it meet a liquidity crisis this avenue towards correcting the liquidity problem is closed to it. Directors should carefully consider the wisdom of taking long-term borrowing up to the theoretical maximum and content themselves with a more modest, but less risky, level of debt.

Consideration should also be given to a wider aspect of using other people's money. Long-term debt is only one way of using other people's money and it may be assumed that the risks associated with borrowing can be avoided by using leasing and hire-purchase. Since leased assets are not owned they do not appear in the balance sheet, although the total leasing payments must be disclosed in the profit and loss account. This means that leasing reduces the value of assets which otherwise would appear in the balance sheet and therefore reduces the company's capacity to raise long-term loans. Further, the annual leasing payments are a fixed charge against the company's profits and therefore increase their vulnerability. If assets are acquired on HP they appear in the balance sheet at the cash price and the amount owing to the HP companies is shown as a liability which other lenders could not ignore. In addition, the HP repayments are a fixed obligation which the company must meet.

Default by the company

The second aspect of long-term debt which must be considered is the possibility that the company will meet a period of poor trading and reduced cash flows that is so severe that it is unable to service interest and loan repayments. The lenders of money try and provide for this contingency by applying adequate earnings and asset cover multiples, but the directors have a duty to ensure that the company does not take on burdens which it might not be able to support. To do this they should:

1. Be aware of the likely limits lenders of money would apply to the company.
2. Ensure that forecasts are prepared of:
   (a) the cash flows available to service debt in normal conditions;
   (b) the cash flows available to service debt in a period of recession.
3. Maintain an adequate margin of debt capacity free to meet possible future contingencies.

The point of crisis

The crisis point can be illustrated using the figures for Incognito Ltd on p. 83. Let us assume that there is a further decline in profitability and liquidity in the following year and that the decline in liquidity is so serious that the board is compelled to consider raising further long-term capital. The directors might first consider the possibility of borrowing more money on a long-term basis. Borrowings are, however, already 34 per cent of the total capital employed and the existing debenture holders have a prior charge on all the assets of the company. In this situation it is quite possible that lenders would decline to provide further funds that would rank after the existing debenture.

The alternative to borrowing is to raise the funds required by a rights issue. If, however, profitability has declined substantially in terms of ROCE the gearing effect will depress the return on equity even further, perhaps to the point where shareholders may prove to be reluctant to take up a rights issue and it would in fact be legally impossible to do so if the share price has slumped to below the par value of the shares.

The company is now at its crisis point. It is exposed to action by its creditors to secure repayment of amounts owing to them. At the same time the avenues by which it can quickly rectify the liquidity position are closed to it. Short-term measures to enable it to survive must be sought, such as paying the more pressing creditors at the expense of the more complaisant ones and using the maximum overdraft facilities. These measures do not change the underlying position, they only put off the evil day and to some extent may make final collapse more certain.

In this situation the board can only pursue three policies and hope that the company can survive until an upturn in profitability can be achieved, thus making it possible to launch a rights issue. These policies are:

1. To reduce the demand for funds to finance stocks and work in progress and debtors.
2. To carry out a reappraisal of operating profitability in all areas with a view to bringing that activity up to an acceptable level of profitability or disposing of it.
3. To reverse the process of over-investment in fixed assets by such acts as the sale and leaseback of premises (if this can be carried out with the consent of the debenture holders), or disposal of unprofitable activities.

It is likely to be a long hard haul before the company is fully recovered and is able to think in terms of expansion once more.

The lesson for directors is that the company need never have been placed in such danger. It is the level of investment in fixed assets allied to expanding sales which has caused the liquidity problem. Either those events were planned by the board, in which case provision of the long-term funds required should have been made earlier, i.e., during years 1 or 2 when it would have been quite feasible to have a rights issue, or they happened fortuitously, in which case the board had little control of their company and were not fully apprised of what was happening.

10.

Operational planning and control

Operational planning is the process of determining in detail what is to be done during the following year. Control is the process of checking performance against the plans and deciding what to do when deviations from the plans begin to show. Planning and control are processes which are carried out at all levels of management. The board of directors is concerned with setting the planning framework for the company as a whole, the lower levels of management have a more restricted task related to their own particular area of responsibility and which must be carried out within the framework of the company plan.

If adequate opportunity is to be given for the fullest amount of management participation, planning should start well before the beginning of the period to which it relates. It is essential that adequate opportunity is provided for discussion and for resolving the various sectional interests both with each other and with the requirements of the company. The more the individual manager is committed to the plans for his responsibility area the more effort he is likely to put into the achievement of whatever targets are set. This requires discussion and perhaps argument before differences are resolved to each manager's satisfaction. While this process can be lengthy there must, of course, be some time limit to the period of discussion or the plans would probably not be approved before the year started.

The timing of the control process must be linked to the requirements of the area being controlled. Some aspects, such as corporate and divisional performance, may be adequately served by monthly control reports and decisions. Other aspects more directly linked to the day-to-day operations, such as shop floor performance or branch sales, may require reports and decisions at intervals much more frequent than one month if they are to be effective.

What is a control system?

In a one-man business formal planning and control are not required because the owner of that business has a direct knowledge of events and results.

Businesses of increasing size require increasingly sophisticated information systems if those who are in a position to control are to exercise that function effectively and the individual activities are to be coordinated towards a common goal. This formal process can be resolved into three parts:

1. Planning to provide a framework of reference.
2. Feedback of information.
3. Comparison of actual performance as revealed by the feedback with planned performance to provide the basis for control decisions.

Perhaps the simplest illustration of a control system is the thermostatically controlled heating system. There is an activity to be controlled, in this case the generation of heat. The standard result that should be achieved by that activity is determined by the setting of the temperature on the thermostat. The feedback of information in this case is the measurement of the actual room temperature and feeding this back to the thermostat. The control process is then quite straightforward. If the actual room temperature exceeds the range provided for in the thermostat setting the heating is switched off— if it falls below the required temperature range the heating is switched on.

A business control system works in very much the same way. There are a number of activities to be controlled; standards of performance are set, such as budgets and standard costs of operations; there is a management accounting system which records and reports upon the different activities; if those reports disclose that any activity is diverging significantly from the standard set there must be a management decision on the response to that divergence. There is one aspect where the business control system does differ from the thermostat system. The latter is designed to bring the temperature at all times within the range set on the thermostat, i.e., to conform to the standard. The business control system has more of an optimizing function. For example, if the level of sales begins to significantly exceed the level provided for in the budget, management would not try to bring the sales performance down to the level budgeted for unless there are specific constraints on volume of production. Management's task in such a situation should be to use the framework provided by the budget to decide what changes should be made in other activities to deal with the increased sales volume, such as increasing production volume, material purchasing, etc.

If the board is to be fully informed of what is happening in the company and to be in a position to control its day-to-day activities, a control system appropriate for that company's particular activities should be installed. The system adopted should be designed to meet the specific needs of the company with the minimum data collection and disturbance to the productive activities.

Planning should be forward looking not backward looking

Planning the framework of activities for the coming year should be based upon translating the long-term strategies into an integrated plan of action for that period. While it must obviously take into account short-term factors, such as the state of the national economy and specific economic factors affecting the industry the company operates in, it must be orientated towards the achievement of the company's long-term objectives and strategy. The first step in the preparation of the annual plans is to determine what needs to be achieved during the year by reference to the long-term plans, and then in association with the managers involved to determine how that is to be carried out.

General management aspects of control systems

In addition to the basic function of the control system to plan and control activities through such methods as budgetary control and setting performance standards, the system can make positive contributions to the overall management process. For example:

—In a diverse organization the various activities can be coordinated and any imbalances minimized.

—Goals or targets can be established for individual managers thus providing a means of assessing manager performance.

—The involvement of managers in planning their area of activity and in securing their backing for the plans approved can be an important aid to motivation, particularly when this is allied to rewarding the manager by reference to his performance against the plans adopted.

—As a detailed statement of operational plans for the company and its constituent units, the budget can make a significant contribution to communication within the company.

It is a management control system

One factor that often limits the effectiveness of the planning and control system is that it is seen by managers and others as a system devised by accountants whereby they can control what happens in the company. This mistaken view arises because the preparation of detailed budgets, the collection and analysis of the information feedback, and the interpretation of deviations from the budgets are in the hands of the accounting staff.

This situation is quite wrong. The system is a *management* system and its function is to aid management in the control of the business or other activity. This it does by providing management with the information that it requires in order to make planning and control decisions. It is management which should decide what values are to be incorporated into plans and what response is to be made where performance deviates from those plans, not accountants. While the latter may be intimately concerned with planning and control and the provision of information, these facilities should be provided merely as a service to management and not to control management. Only where the accountant is acting as a manager, either as a departmental head or in managing one of the corporate responsibility centres, such as corporate liquidity control, do planning and control decisions become his direct responsibility—and then because he is functioning as a manager, not as an accountant.

The attitude of directors will have a large influence on the way the rest of the company's personnel regard the planning and control system. If the board exercise the control function via the accounting network, as, for example, asking the head of the finance function to report directly to the board on the variances from budget and the action that is proposed to deal with such variances, then the system is likely to be regarded as representing control by the accountants. This can be avoided if the directors ensure that managers alone are held accountable for performance in their responsibility area, that requests for information or explanation of variances are addressed directly to the manager, and that he alone should be responsible for reporting on his area of activity to the board. The accounting function would then be merely an aid to the manager in dealing with the requirements of the planning and control system.

The director's role

The effectiveness of the planning and control system has a direct effect upon the capacity of directors to discharge their responsibilities for controlling the future activities of the company and its day-to-day operations. The larger the business the more difficult is that task unless the director can rely upon a structured system which provides him with the necessary information. The board should take a critical look at proposals for new control systems and from time to time critically review existing systems. In particular the directors should ask themselves:

1. Is there an adequate information base upon which they can make proper judgements on which to base plans for the following year? They need not only the long-term plan requirements but also information on short-term aspects which must be allowed for.
2. Do managers have the appropriate information for planning their own responsibility area activities? They need for this an understanding of the requirements of the company's overall plans for their area of operation and, where appropriate, the way in which external factors may affect their operations during the year.
3. Has the budget preparation process been structured in such a way that, as far as is possible, managers agree their budgets and do not have them imposed upon them? The ultimate decision must be at the top but the commitment of managers to their budget must be gained as far as possible.
4. Will the performance standards represented by budgets and operating standards give an adequate measure of the manager's or operator's effort

over the period? If managers and others are to be rewarded on the basis of performance against budget or another standard, a situation where a manager can put in little effort and still meet the requirements of his budget and another manager can work extremely hard and still fall short of budget must be avoided as far as possible. Events during the year may make it either harder or easier to meet the requirements of budgets and some attempt must be made to assess such factors and the effect that they would have on manager performance so that this can be incorporated into the final appraisal.

5. Is the control system designed to provide directors and managers with the right reports at the right time? The feedback of information must be related to the time interval of control. For example, if operating standards have been set for each step in the production of a product with a short manufacturing time cycle, the foreman or superintendant responsible for the department(s) engaged in making that product may well require daily reports on operating effciency so that he can take immediate corrective action and is not required to wait several weeks before he knows his department's current operating efficiency.

6. Is sufficient time set aside in the planning process for directors to make a critical review of the plans before they receive final approval? Directors have a duty at this stage to question the assumptions on which the budgets have been based—even assumptions which they themselves have made in the early stages of planning. Only when all the budgets have been prepared and summarized can they be tested to see whether they meet the requirements of long-term planning and specific goals, such as ROCE. It is also necessary to see that the cash flows that would emerge if the budget is met are adequate and that the company is in a position to raise any extra capital that would be required. In this connection the directors should examine possible adjustments to the budget to take account of the economic trade-offs between different aspects of operations, such as the reduction in stock levels to reduce cash demands and increase the turnover of capital employed at the expense of lost sales and profit.

The effectiveness of the system adopted depends to some extent on the commitment of the directors to the system. If managers see decisions being taken without reference to the system, then it will tend to become a formality which must be observed but which is unlikely to play a major role in their own decision taking. In such a situation unofficial information systems will be set up by managers and others to justify their decisions and to use as a basis for proposals to the board.

Directors should also see the planning process as a medium for searching for alternative, better ways of achieving the objectives of the company. A mechanistic approach to planning which accepts company practices in an uncritical way is not conducive to efficient operating practices. Those concerned with planning should be encouraged to question all proposals and to feel free to make radical suggestions for change.

What must directors control?

The essential factors which should be included in any company's control system are those which have a direct effect on the viability of that company. These may vary to some extent from company to company and in their relative importance. What might be the most critical features for a food retailing chain might be quite different from those for a high technology company or one producing high volume unsophisticated products. Common to all companies, however, is the need to control the principal factors which affect profitability and liquidity including the level of investment in fixed and other assets. Some of these factors are discussed below.

Overall company profit and loss

The function of this area of control is to ensure that an adequate sales volume is attained and that the levels of cost incurred are kept to a minimum in relation to that sales volume so that the residue of sales value left as profit is adequate for the company's needs. The emphasis may vary from company to company. In some, sales volume and margins may be more critical, whereas in others operating efficiency, as reflected in the level of costs, may be more important.

Performance at cost/profit centre

The board needs to control not only overall performance, but also performance in each of the principal management responsibility centres. Satisfactory overall company performance does not necessarily mean that all parts of the business are operating properly. The directors need to know each manager's responsibility for sales performance, for specific departmental cost items, and for overall profit performance, and have the facility in the operating budgetary control system to see how individual managers are performing.

Performance at shop floor, retail outlet, or service level

These are areas which are the prime responsibility of line managers who will normally be the recipients of the detailed data on performance within their fields of responsibility. The director requires an overall appraisal of performance at these levels so that he can ensure that the line managers concerned are carrying out their duties properly. The director also requires direct information on the key activities of the company, e.g., such matters as sales and gross profit per square foot of display space, the cost per activity (such as the cost of preparing insurance renewal notices or invoices), or worker efficiency (such as the actual time taken to produce the actual output against the time it should have taken in accordance with some pre-determined standard).

Product costs

The knowledge of what a product or service costs is an essential ingredient of management decisions and in planning future activities. What level of costs is relevant for particular decisions is dealt with in chapter 12. The cost analysis used for budgets should take into account the type of analysis that may be required for product or service costing. Not only is it essential to control product costs but also to set up an early-warning system for cost changes so that prices can be adjusted at the earliest possible time.

Cash flow and liquidity

Directors need to be aware of the cash flow consequences of their plans and to be in a position to control the day-to-day cash position and appreciate the cash consequences when other operating activities diverge from the budget. At all times they should be aware of the current cash position and the likely future cash flows.

Movements in investment

Cash flow and liquidity are affected directly by changes in the level of investment in fixed and current assets. Changes in these values must therefore be subject to the planning and control process. Stocks and work in progress and debtors, being short-term assets, can be planned as a part of the overall operating plans and any cash flow consequences incorporated into the cash budgeting. Information on movements in the levels of investment should be available to the directors and an assessment of how effectively the control system operates, expressed in the form of ratios discussed in chapter 7.

The pattern of investment in fixed assets determines future profitability and the level of such investment directly affects liquidity. The control system set up should enable the directors to:

1. Control the total level of expenditure on fixed assets over a three- to five-year period.
2. Assess the effect that individual investment proposals would have on profitability at ROCE level.

It must be emphasized that the ability of the directors to control fixed investment is limited to the period *before* the investment is made. Once the company's funds have been committed to a fixed use in this way the opportunity to control has gone. If the wrong decision has been made the company must either retain the asset and live with the consequences in terms of lower operating efficiency or dispose of it and accept any losses on disposal. This is a key decision area since it determines where large slices of the company's funds are to be invested and locks them into those uses on a long-term basis.

The directors must be directly involved in making such decisions for major investments and for controlling the pattern of minor investments.

The operating budget

What determines the level of activity for the following year? In most cases the volume of activity is determined by the ability of the company to sell its products and it is this that sets the pattern for other activities, such as purchasing and production. In other cases there may be constraints on volume arising from such factors as physical limitations to the productive capacity or financial constraints. In such a case the starting point for budget preparation would be to determine what the limit to volume is and, as a consequence, what is the best mix of products or services to sell to fill that capacity.

This definition of the factor which limits the company's scale of operations is an important one and one in which the directors should be involved. It will have considerable impact on the way financial data is used in decision making as well as affecting the preparation of the operating budgets.

The sales budget

Assuming that the ability to sell is the only factor that limits the company's operations, the first stage in budget preparation is to plan the likely level of sales so that the demands upon purchasing, production and other resources can be assessed. In establishing that plan, management can have recourse to such information sources as:
—Requirements of the long-term plan.
—Extrapolation of previous years' sales.
—General and industry economic trends.
—Estimates by sales field staff.
—Planned promotional activities.
—Forecast competition trends.
—Market research.
—Population trends.

At the end of the sales planning activity there should emerge for the next stages of planning:
—What products are to be sold in what volumes.
—The trend in sales volume of each product over the budget period so that monthly or other period budgets can be prepared.
—The volume of each product to be sold in different markets or through different distribution channels.
—What changes in finished goods stock are required to support changing sales volumes.

An illustration of a sales budget is given at the end of the chapter in Table 10.1, section B. It is based upon Incognito Ltd whose last three years' accounts were used for the ratio analysis in chapter 7. The budgets illustrated in Table 10.1 are for the year immediately following the period covered by the ratio analysis.

The production budget

Planned level of activity

In any situation where a company produces the goods that it sells it must prepare a production budget. The planned level of production for each product is based upon the budgeted level of sales for those products in the sales budget. The values used in the sales budget must be adjusted, however, for any planned changes in the levels of finished stocks. The way in which changes in the stock levels are planned depends upon the relative desirability of achieving a balanced production volume over the whole year and that of minimizing the level of investment in stocks.

Planning direct production costs

Where the direct cost per unit of each product or service is known in terms of unit material cost, unit direct labour cost, and any other direct costs, the total planned expenditure on materials, direct wages and other direct costs is a simple process of multiplying the volume of each product per month by the unit direct costs. For example, in Table 10.1 the production plan envisages the production of 7000 units of product A in January. The expected material costs for that product are £3.20 per unit. The total material costs for that product, in this case the material Floro, for that month would be £3.20 × 7000 which amounts to the £22 400 in the direct production costs for that material in January.

Where the business does not sell standardized products or services, estimates must be made of the likely level of expenditure on direct costs—such estimates being based upon past experience, possible changes in product mix, changing production patterns, etc., or any other basis which might be more appropriate.

Indirect costs

Planning must now concentrate upon the indirect costs that are required to support the production volume planned. This covers such costs as indirect labour costs, rent and rates of the factory, heat and light, power, repairs and maintenance, etc. The budgeting process is likely to be centred upon the departmental or other structure of the manufacturing organization. Thus each departmental manager would be required to plan in budget form his departmental expenditure on indirect costs. These would be scrutinized at a higher level and when agreed aggregated to form the functional budget for manufacturing.

Where the company is structured in such a way that there are a number of central service functions operating under separate managers the costs of which must be distributed to the departments or divisions using their services, the manufacturing functional budget would have to include the appropriate share of such costs.

The production budget for Incognito Ltd shown in Table 10.1 at the end of this chapter is based upon the manufacture of two products. Production is scheduled on the basis that there should be at least a two-month lead time before sale, so that effectively two months' stock is maintained at all times for each of the products. No changes are planned in material stocks or in work in progress, therefore the scheduling of material purchases can be made on the basis of simply replacing the materials which are scheduled to be used in production in each of the months.

The direct production costs are the multiple of the quantity of each product to be produced each month and the unit direct costs. The structure of the indirect production costs is basically a matrix of type of cost and managerial responsibility for the cost. The cost classification adopted should meet the requirements of the company's financial and cost accounting systems so that conflicts and misunderstanding are minimized. The structure of managerial responsibility depends upon the organizational framework in the manufacturing function and the responsibility for budgets should adhere to this as far as is possible.

Note that the example shown in Table 10.1 distinguishes between *controllable* costs and *non-controllable* costs. Controllable in this context means whether or not the person in whose budget the cost appears is in a position to control spending of that type or not. For example, the share of building occupancy costs shown on a departmental manager's budget does not lie within his control. He cannot overspend or restrict expenditure in that area but is entirely dependent upon decisions taken by others.

This distinction is an important one from the control point of view as it is unrealistic to make a person responsible for controlling costs which he cannot influence. The control system is likely to function more effectively if the responsibility of a manager for cost control is limited to those items which are affected by his decisions. The balance of the costs should be the responsibility of general management or the person who is responsible for that area of costs, e.g., the occupancy of buildings.

The selling and distribution budget

This section of the operating budget includes all those costs incurred from the point at which the product leaves the manufacturing process until they are in the hands of the company's customers. It includes such expense items as sales force salaries and expenses, promotions and advertising, market research, physical distribution, warehousing, retail outlets, etc.

The importance of this part of the budget varies considerably with the type of business that the company undertakes. In some types of manufacturing activity the sales costs are relatively small and require little control. Other manufacturing companies who sell direct to a wide clientele may find that the selling costs form the majority of the company's expenditure and require control even more than do manufacturing costs. Companies, such as supermarket chains, being wholly orientated to selling must plan and control this group of costs as part of its principal control activity—control in this case being centered upon measuring in some way the cost effectiveness of the different groups of expenditure and in different outlets against the volume of sales achieved, since this is the relationship which is critical for this type of activity. Whatever the degree of importance of the sales budget one of the principal elements to be taken into account in its preparation is the volume of sales planned in the sales budget. This directly determines some types of expenditure, e.g., commissions on sales, and has an indirect effect on other expenses which tend to vary with the volume of sales, such as travelling expenses.

Administration budget

This part of the operating budget includes the costs of those departments which serve the company as an entity rather than a single function. It includes such departments as accounting and personnel and carries the general management costs of the board of directors and senior executives.

Budgeted company profit and loss account

Once the various functional budgets have been prepared they are brought together in the normal profit and loss account format. This would show the company's profit performance for the year if the company works exactly to budget. For Incognito Ltd the position is shown in section F of Table 10.1. The sales value is that included in the sales budget and the cost of sales is arrived at by totalling the production costs for the year and deducting from that total the value of the increases in finished goods stocks that are planned. This is the only adjustment required in this case as material stocks and work in progress are planned to remain constant. Where this is not the case, suitable adjustments will have to be provided to manufacturing costs to arrive at the cost of sales for the period.

The value of the increased level of finished stocks is arrived at by adopting full manufacturing costs as the basis for stock valuation. It therefore comprises the direct material and labour costs and the appropriate part of the manufacturing overhead costs. Assuming that Incognito recovers overheads as a rate per labour hour the overhead rate would be £2·523 per labour hour.[1]

[1] Total production hours = A 123 000 units × 6 hours   738 000
                             B 86 000 units × 4 hours   344 000
                                                             1 082 000

$$\text{overhead rate } \frac{\pounds 2\ 730\ 000}{1\ 082\ 000 \text{ hours}} = \pounds 2\text{·}523$$

The cost would therefore be as follows for product A:

		£
Direct materials		3·2
Direct labour		7·2
Overheads—6 hrs @ £2·523 per hour		15·14
		25·54

The critical review

On the basis of the assumptions used in preparing the budget the company would have an operating profit of £465 000 and a pre-tax profit of £315 000 against the corresponding values for the previous year of £767 000 and £617 000. If the budget is adopted in its present form it implies that management is accepting a sharply declining level of profitability. In its review of the budget the board should question whether the assumptions upon which it is based are valid and whether there are areas where costs could be cut, sales revenue increased, or operating practices changed.

As a first step in its review the board might well compare the budget for the coming year with the results of past years along the following lines:

	Year 1	Year 2	Year 3	Budget for Year 4
	(percentage of sales values)			
Sales	100·0	100·0	100·0	100·0
Cost of sales	66·7	64·5	70·7	78·7
Gross profit	33·3	35·5	29·3	21·3
Operating expenses	17·4	15·7	14·8	13·7
Operating profit	15·9	19·8	14·5	7·6
Interest	—	3·2	2·8	2·4
Net profit	15·9	16·6	11·7	5·2

The above analysis clearly shows that the problem lies with the high level of manufacturing costs and the effect that this is having upon the gross profit margin. Compared with the previous year the proportion of sales value absorbed by manufacturing costs has increased from 70·7 per cent to 78·7 per cent. With the exception of year 2 there is evidence of a long-term trend towards higher production costs in relation to selling price. Management must determine whether this is due to manufacturing inefficiency, rising material costs, or setting selling prices too low. Whatever the cause, this is a critical problem for the company. If the same movement in gross profit margins takes place in the next year the company will make a loss. The operating expenses have a favourable trend. Had this not been the case the components of operating expenses should have been segregated so that the adverse elements could have been identified and investigated.

The capital budget

In the process of drawing up the operating budget it may become apparent that the company requires additional physical resources in terms of buildings, plant and machinery, etc. Managers may also have made suggestions for the replacement of ageing plant or the introduction of cost-saving equipment. The final outline of likely new investment in fixed assets should be tested against the long-term plan to ensure that the pattern of investment is in accordance with those plans.

Management's task is to ensure that the most effective use is made of the scarce resource of capital and that the level of expenditure on fixed assets does not jeopardize the liquidity of the company. This necessitates in addition to the detailed budget for the coming year a longer-term look at the total annual expenditure required. In the case of Incognito Ltd management expects the expenditure for the following year to be £600 000 spread evenly over the whole year.

Cash budget and projected balance sheet

The budgeting process is completed by the preparation of a cash budget and constructing the balance sheet of the company as it would appear if the company performs exactly to standard. The importance of this part of the total budgeting process cannot be overemphasized and lack of attention to it can have critical consequences. The introduction of a balance sheet at the end of the planning year also enables the plans to be examined by means of the ratios used in chapter 7 so that management can follow not only past trends, but also compare them with the projected results for the year ahead. This should form a major element in management's critical appraisal of the budgets before they are approved. Because of their importance they are dealt with separately in the next chapter.

Product costing

In addition to being analysed by type of expense or by the operating area in which they are incurred, expenses can also be analysed by the product or service for which they were incurred. Many important decision areas can only be dealt with rationally if management is aware of the costs of each of the products or services that it provides. How those decisions can be made is dealt with in chapter 12. The board must, however, give some consideration to the product or service cost information that it requires for control purposes and how this can be linked to the special requirements of such information when it is used for decision taking.

TABLE 10.1
Budgets for Incognito Ltd for year 4

Section A– product cost information

	Product A Last year £	Product A Forecast £		Product B Last year £	Product B Forecast £
Direct materials:					
2 lb Floro @ 160p per lb	3·20	3·20	6 lb Exo @ 110p per lb	6·60	6·60
Direct labour:					
6 hrs @ 100p per hour	6·00		4 hrs @ 120p per hour	4·80	
6 hrs @ 120p per hour		7·20	4 hrs @ 140p per hour		5·60
Total direct costs	9·20	10·40		11·40	12·20
Selling price	£30			£32	

Section B– the sales plan

	Jan.	Feb.	March	April	May	June	July	Aug.	Sept.	Oct.	Nov.	Dec.	Total
Product A	5 000	4 000	7 000	9 000	14 000	15 000	16 000	13 000	10 000	10 000	8 000	7 000	118 000 units
Product B	5 000	5 000	6 000	6 000	6 000	7 000	7 000	7 000	7 000	8 000	8 000	8 000	80 000 units
Values of sales (£000s)													
Product A	150	120	210	270	420	450	480	390	300	300	240	210	3 540
Product B	160	160	192	192	192	224	224	224	224	256	256	256	2 560
Total	310	280	402	462	612	674	704	614	524	556	496	466	6 100

Section C– the production plan

1. Planned changes in finished stock: both products are to be produced two months before planned sale and it is assumed that the December sales volumes will be continued into the new year.
2. The production schedule

Product A	7 000	9 000	14 000	15 000	16 000	13 000	10 000	10 000	8 000	7 000	7 000	123 000 units
Product B	6 000	6 000	6 000	7 000	7 000	7 000	7 000	8 000	8 000	8 000	8 000	86 000 units

3. Direct expenditure on production[1]

(£000s)

Direct materials												
Floro	22·4	28·8	44·8	48·0	51·2	41·6	32·0	32·0	25·6	22·4	22·4	393·6
Exo	39·6	39·6	39·6	46·2	46·2	46·2	46·2	52·8	52·8	52·8	52·8	567·6
Total	62·0	68·4	84·4	94·2	97·4	87·8	78·2	84·8	78·4	75·2	75·2	961·2
Direct labour												
Product A	50·4	64·8	100·8	108·0	115·2	93·6	72·0	72·0	57·6	50·4	50·4	885·6
Product B	33·6	33·6	33·6	39·2	39·2	39·2	39·2	44·8	44·8	44·8	44·8	481·6
Total	84·0	98·4	134·4	147·2	154·4	132·8	111·2	116·8	102·4	95·2	95·2	1 367·2

[1] We are assuming that materials stocks and work in progress remain constant during the period.

Table 10.1 Section C continued

4. Indirect production costs

			Responsibility centre			
Type of expense	Production management	Production planning	Storekeeping	etc.	etc.	Total
	£	£	£	£	£	£000s
Controllable						
Supervision salaries	8 870	4 600	1 980	x x x	x x x	195
Other salaries	10 460	32 100	9 760	x x x	x x x	320
Weekly wages	3 200	9 800	10 460	x x x	x x x	148
Repairs and maintenance	300	200	400	x x x	x x x	94
Stationery	1 100	3 200	4 600	x x x	x x x	23
Travelling expenses	800	300	100	x x x	x x x	5
etc.	x x x	x x x	x x x	x x x	x x x	x x x
etc.	x x x	x x x	x x x	x x x	x x x	x x x
Total controllable	34 000	64 500	49 600	x x x	x x x	1 688
Non-controllable						
Depreciation	220 900	1 500	—	x x x	x x x	330
Rent and rates	168 400	9 600	1 700	—	—	312
etc.	x x x	x x x	x x x	x x x	x x x	x x x
etc.	x x x	x x x	x x x	x x x	x x x	x x x
Total indirect expenses	421 000	102 500	68 700	x x x	x x x	2 730

Section D – selling and distribution expenses

			Responsibility centre			
Type of expenses	Sales manager	Warehouse	Transport	Marketing	etc.	Total
	£	£	£	£	£	£000s
Management salaries	10 000	5 000	6 000	12 000	x x x	42
Salesmen's salaries	169 000	—	—	—	—	169
Other salaries	34 000	12 500	11 600	33 200	x x x	98
Travelling expenses	24 000	1 200	1 500	3 500	x x x	34
Commission	34 320	—	—	—	—	34
Vehicle running costs	—	—	26 000	—	—	26
Depreciation	3 000	12 500	9 000	—	—	34
etc.	x x x x	x x x x x	x x x x x	x x x x x	x x x x x	x x
Total selling and distribution expenses	316 000	41 200	63 000	51 200	x x x x x x x	634

Section E – Administration expenses

			Responsibility centre			
Type of expense	Secretary	Accounts	Personnel	etc.	etc.	Total
	£	£	£	£	£	£000s
Director's fees	2 000	—	—	—	—	2
Management salaries	9 380	12 190	13 800	x x x x	x x x	51
Other salaries	3 600	19 800	12 500	x x x x	x x x x	69
Stationery	630	13 460	2 980	x x x x	x x x x	20
Telephone	240	1 300	1 190	x x x x	x x x x	7
Depreciation	2 110	4 023	1 820	x x x x	x x x x	24
etc.	x x x	x x x	x x x	x x x x x	x x x	x x x
Total administration expenses	47 200	63 200	34 000	x x x x x	x x x x x	204

Section F– profit and loss account

		£000s	£000s
Budgeted sales			6 100
Budgeted cost of sales:			
Manufacturing expenses: Direct materials		961	
Direct labour		1 367	
Indirect manufacturing expenses		2 730	
		5 058	
Less: Planned increase in finished stock:			
5000 units increase in A @ £25·54 per unit	127·7		
6000 units increase in B @ £22·29 per unit	133·7		
		261	
			4 797
Gross profit			1 303
Selling and distribution expenses		634	
Administration expenses		204	
			838
Operating profit			465
Interest			150
			315
Net profit before tax			315

11.

Cash flow planning and control

Why cash planning and control?

In a sense cash is the ultimate resource for a business. Without it the business is unable to acquire the other resources that it needs to continue in business. Lack of cash can put the existence of the company at risk. Directors have a duty, therefore, to ensure that the company that they manage has enough cash available at all times to meet its day-to-day requirements. The cash should be available not most of the time but *all* of the time if the company is not to be put at risk of collapsing if cash non-availability occurs at a time when raising new capital might be impossible.

The cash budget which results from the planning activity is also an essential element in the negotiation of overdraft facilities from the company's bankers. It forms the basis for forecasting the amount of bank facilities required and demonstrates that the company will be able to repay the overdraft within any time scale required by the bank.

The requirements for presentation of cash budgets to the company's banker should be kept in mind when they are prepared. The need to maintain the best relations with the company's bankers has been stressed in chapter 5. Whether or not the company keeps within the budgets that it sets, and adheres to the bank's terms for advancing money, contributes considerably to the bank's view of the efficiency of the management. To this end requests for overdraft facilities should not be pared down to the bone, thus increasing the possibility of having to go back to the bank at a later date to negotiate a higher figure. Any requests for overdraft facilities should also cover all possible contingencies so that it would require a major upset in forecasts to make the company exceed its loan limits. Uncertainties in the cash budget, i.e., when an occurrence or its timing is uncertain, the uncertainty should be resolved in the cash budget by taking the item in at its worst position which would mean bringing it in at the earliest time it might occur.

While much of the detailed work of cash flow planning and control can be delegated by the directors to appropriate management staff, they do have a duty to ensure that the methods applied are effective and also to appreciate that the decisions they are taking in other areas may directly affect cash flow. The achievement of other plans and objectives can only be secured if the financial resources are adequate. In their appreciation of proposed operating plans the directors must, before approving them, satisfy themselves that the cash requirements to support the activities are known, and that suitable arrangements have been made for the necessary cash to be made available, whether by long-term funding or by the arrangement of short-term facilities, such as bank overdrafts.

To approve the operating budget without ensuring that sufficient cash will be available, and to hope that when the need emerges the necessary cash will be forthcoming from the bank or other source, is to court disaster. Moreover, when the operating budget has been approved and is backed up with adequate financial resources if, during the course of the budget control period, significant deviations from the planned activities occur, an appreciation must be made of the effect that those deviations may have on the planned cash flows. If this appreciation indicates that the cash flows will be adversely affected steps should be taken to increase the funding of the company if this is considered proper by the directors. If the directors do not want to increase the funding of the company or it is impossible because of the state of the financial markets, then changes must be made in other parts of the operating plan to keep the net cash flows within the original constraints.

There can be no short cut to cash flow planning. It can only be through the possession of a detailed knowledge of the cash flow consequences of every activity within the company that the cash plan can be prepared. Effective control, then, can only be achieved by monitoring current cash flows and ensuring that there is an immediate feedback of information on matters which may affect future cash flows. A knowledge of the current cash position and future cash flow trends is the cornerstone of good cash control.

Major factors which affect cash flow

Understanding the factors which affect cash needs is a first step in cash control since it is only through control of such factors that the cash flow itself can be controlled. In other words, cash flows are a consequence of what is happening in the business, they do not happen of their own accord and it is these originators of cash flows which must be tackled at source.

As in other planning activities, cash flow planning begins with the long-term requirements of the corporate strategy. While profit orientated day-to-day management on an operating unit basis is important, it is the long-term decisions which cause large gains or losses. The long-term alternatives must be weighed up and economic trade-offs considered as well as potential risks. Many managements of large companies view the company as comprising a portfolio of investments in major operating units each of which operates in an independent market for its goods or services. Each unit has its own objectives and strategies for achieving those objectives. In such a business, corporate management's task is to ensure that the portfolio comprises a mix of operating units which improves returns in relation to risks, and balances funds usage with funds generation and ability to raise new capital, thereby ensuring the survival of the company.

The sources and applications of funds statement required by SSAP 1O to be included with the annual financial report is a historical analysis of those factors that have affected the company's cash resources over the past year. This statement will be more meaningful to its users if it is divided up in a way that shows:
1. Funds generated by operations.
2. Funds generated from financial resources.
3. Funds invested, repaid or distributed.
This division separates the responsibility for funds flows since those funds flows included in 1 are the responsibility of operating unit managers and those in 2 and 3 are the result of corporate management decisions.

Directors should decide what the cash movements for the same items are likely to be for the following years. In particular, the matters discussed below should receive critical attention.

Changes in the collection period for debtors

Movements in the collection period for debtors directly affect cash flows. Each day's slippage in collection period increases the cash required to finance debtors by the equivalent of one day's credit sales. In the case of Incognito Ltd, each change of one day in the collection period represents a change in the cash required to finance debtors of £15 000.

Changes in the turnover of stocks and work in progress

An increase in stocks and work-in-progress levels is an indication that current expenditure on labour and material costs is not all going to be recouped from sales revenue in the near future, but will have to be carried forward and financed by the company until such time as the stocks can be sold. Control depends upon the effectiveness of the stock control procedures and upon ensuring that sales volume and production and/or purchasing volumes are kept in balance. The implications for cash flow of changes in the rate at which stocks, etc., are turned over can be seen for Incognito Ltd on p. 87. If in the second of the years the rate of stock turnover had been maintained at the 4·22 times turnover achieved in the first year, the stock value would only have been £723 000 instead of the actual value of £1 136 000. In other words, some £400 000 more of the company's funds have been locked up in this use than was warranted by the increase in sales volume. This is a significant claim on the cash resources of a business of the size illustrated.

Changes in the level of business

Planned increases in levels of sales are, of course, a welcome trend in any business. They should, however, be treated with caution, since almost inevitably such a change will substantially increase the cash requirements of the company. Extra stock must be purchased to support the higher sales, debtors increase in line with the extra sales, both of which usually happen before the cash flows begin to benefit from the higher sales volume. Remember that the first effect of an upsurge in sales is an outflow of cash. Overtrading, i.e., trying to support too high a level of activity on too small a capital base, is a major cause of the liquidation of companies.

Seasonality of the business

A business with strong seasonal influences is likely to have wide swings in cash requirements over the year, quite apart from demands for cash resulting from an underlying upward trend in sales volume. Stocks may be built up before the seasonal peak and there is a strong possibility that the amount of debtors will vary considerably. Management usually has a choice where the company is affected by seasonal factors. One policy may be to keep stocks level and adjust the production rate to the seasonal demand. The other is to keep production rates steady over the period and meet the seasonal variation in demand by increasing and running down stocks. Cash requirements to meet seasonal cash peaks are short term and are usually covered by bank borrowing.

Expenditure on fixed assets

The level of expenditure on fixed assets directly affects cash flow and, as was shown in chapter 9, can also affect the financial stability of the company.

Dividend policy

While in a sense the dividend can be adjusted to the then existing cash availability, major fluctuations in dividends paid can have undesirable effects upon the company's share price. The directors should therefore pursue as far as is possible a consistent dividend policy. The drain on cash arising from dividend payments is not confined to the dividend itself. There is also the requirement to pay ACT to cover the amount of the tax credits associated with the dividend. While ACT may be eventually recovered by way of an offset against the mainstream corporation tax payment, in the interim it is effectively a forced loan to the government.

Directors' responsibilities

The directors' duties with regard to the planning and control of cash flow can only be adequately carried out if they ensure that:

1. The long-term and short-term funds generation and investment of each operating unit are known and matched with the ability of the company to raise new capital.
2. A cash budget is prepared and it is in accordance with the operating and other budgets.
3. Any perceived cash deficiencies are covered by bank or other borrowing.
4. There is an effective reporting of actual cash movements against the budget, and current bank balances.
5. Events which may result in major cash movements not included in the budget are reported immediately.
6. A strategy for maintaining the best possible relations with the company's bankers is identified and put into practice.

What is a cash budget?

The cash budget is a summary of all cash movements, both payments and receipts, expected to occur during the planning period in their appropriate time periods. That is to say that the budget is based on when the actual receipt or payment will take place. It includes all the cash flow consequences of the items of income and expenditure which appear in the operating budget, together with cash flows for matters not appearing in that budget, such as capital expenditure, loan repayments, taxation, dividends, etc.

The cash budget for Incognito Ltd is shown in Table 11.1. It is based upon the following assumptions.

1. Credit to customers will be limited to two months on average, and during the first two months of the year all amounts due at the end of the previous year will be collected.
2. Payments for material purchases are made four months after purchase. £240 000 of the creditors at the end of the previous year are in respect of materials, with the balance of £195 000 relating to other purchases, and this amount is not expected to change over the year.
3. Capital expenditure will total £600 000 spread evenly over the year.
4. Current tax is payable on 1 January.
5. The final dividend for last year will be paid in March and an interim dividend for the current year will be paid in October at the same rate as that in the previous year.
6. Interest on the loan is paid half-yearly in June and December.

In order not to over-complicate the example shown for Incognito, certain refinements have been omitted. In practice, for example, salaries and wages would be shown net in the month of payment and the related PAYE and social security payments in the following month. The dividend and interest payments are both shown in net terms, but in later months there would be payments of ACT and payments in respect of tax deducted from interest. Major periodic payments, such as rent and rate payments, would be segre-

TABLE 11.1
Cash budget for Incognito Ltd (£000s)

	Jan.	Feb.	March	April	May	June	July	Aug.	Sept.	Oct.	Nov.	Dec.	Total
Cash in													
Product A	525	525	150	120	210	270	420	450	480	390	300	300	
Product B			160	160	192	192	192	224	224	224	224	256	
Total	525	525	310	280	402	462	612	674	704	614	524	556	6188
Cash out													
Material purchases	60	60	60	60	62	68	85	94	97	88	78	85	897
Wages	84	98	135	147	154	133	111	117	102	95	95	96	1367
Production overheads	200	200	200	200	200	200	200	200	200	200	200	200	2400
Selling and distribution expenses	50	50	50	50	50	50	50	50	50	50	50	50	600
Administration expenses	15	15	15	15	15	15	15	15	15	15	15	15	180
Capital expenditure	50	50	50	50	50	50	50	50	50	50	50	50	600
Corporation tax	390												390
Dividends			140							136			276
Interest						75						75	150
	849	473	650	522	531	591	511	526	514	634	488	571	6860
Net cash in/(out) for month	(324)	52	(340)	(242)	(129)	(129)	101	148	190	(20)	36	(15)	(672)
Cash balance brought forward	(241)	(565)	(513)	(853)	(1095)	(1224)	(1353)	(1252)	(1104)	(914)	(934)	(898)	
Cash balance/(deficit) end of month	(565)	(513)	(853)	(1095)	(1224)	(1353)	(1252)	(1104)	(914)	(934)	(898)	(913)	

gated from other payments and scheduled for payment in the appropriate period.

The first part of Incognito's cash budget schedules the cash that should be received from customers. The receipts for the first two months are based upon the debtors in the company's balance sheet at the end of year 3 on p. 83. As stated in 1 above, all amounts owing to the company at the beginning of the year should be collected in the first two months. Thereafter the monthly collection from sales relate to the sales of two months previously. This means that debtors at the end of the year must be the sales made in November and December. If the company sells on a cash basis, or a mixture of credit and cash sales, the cash sales should be segregated, the cash receipts being scheduled in the same period as the sales. If cash receipts from other sources are expected during the year they should be scheduled in this section of the cash budget. For example, if it were proposed to raise a new loan, or to dispose of some fixed assets, the receipts from such sources would be scheduled in the appropriate period.

The section scheduling cash payments starts with the payments in respect of material purchases. Of the £435 000 owing to creditors at the end of year 19 x 3, £240 000 was for materials and the balance in respect of other purchases on credit. As materials are paid for four months in arrear the payment of this £240 000 is spread over the first four months. Thereafter the monthly payments are based upon the value of materials purchased four months previously. This means that the amount owing to creditors at the end of the year will be the £195 000 for other expenses (which is not expected to change over the year) plus the purchases of materials in the last four months which would still be owing.

The total payments for wages, selling and distribution overheads, and administration expenses are based upon the total expenses included in the operating budget except that depreciation is excluded from each of the totals since there is no cash outlay in respect of the depreciation expense. The payments for capital expenditure are as narrated in the text, as are dividends and interest.

When the totals of the cash receipts and payments each month have been ascertained, the difference between them represents a net cash inflow or net cash outlay each month. In January there is a net cash outflow of £324 000 and to this must be added the bank overdraft brought forward from year 19 x 3 of £241 000. This means that the overdraft by the end of January will reach £565 000—the value shown in the last line of the Table for January. This figure is adjusted for the deficit or surplus in cash movements in each of the following months to show the total deficit or surplus at the end of that month. From the Table it can be seen that the maximum cash requirement occurs in June when the total shortfall in cash would amount to £1 353 000 compared with the requirements at the end of the year of only £913 000. The company would have to make sure that it could arrange finance to cover the £1 353 000 cash requirement before the operating budget could be approved for the year.

The projected balance sheet

The directors' view of the budgets for the year should be completed by the presentation of the balance sheet values as they would appear if the company exactly meets its operating budget and other planned activities during the year. It is helpful if directors appreciate the relationship between the operating budget, the cash budget, and the projected balance sheet at the end of the budget period. The change in the balance sheet value for any item between the beginning and end of the budget period (in the case of Incognito between 31 December 19 × 3 and 31 December 19 × 4) is represented by differences between the value for that item included in the operating budget and that included in the cash budget.

TABLE 11.2

Projected balance sheet for Incognito Ltd at end of budget period (£000s)

	End of budget period 31 Dec. 19 × 4		Actual 31 Dec. 19 × 3	
Uses of funds				
Fixed assets (net)		3574		3362
Current assets:				
Stocks and work in progress	1464		1203	
Debtors	962		1050	
Cash	—		130	
	——	2426	——	2383
		——		——
Less:		6000		5745
Current liabilities:				
Creditors	499		435	
Taxation	309		390	
Dividends	140		140	
Bank overdraft	913		371	
	——	1861	——	1336
		——		——
Net Assets		4139		4409
		——		——
Financed by–				
Shareholders' funds:				
Share capital		1000		1000
Capital reserves		865		865
Retained profits		617		735
		——		——
		2482		2600
10% debenture		1500		1500
Deferred taxation		157		309
		——		——
		4139		4409
		══		══

This can be illustrated by the movement in debtors in the balance sheets in Table 11.2. Debtors at 31 December 19 × 3 amounted to 1 050 000 to which must be added the credit sales included in the operating budget of £6 100 000. The cash collection from debtors is planned in the cash budget as £6 188 000. This would leave owing at the end of the year £962 000, the amount shown in the projected balance sheet at 31 December 19 × 4. Less obvious is the relationship between the values for fixed assets in the two balance sheets. These can be reconciled in the following manner:

	£000s
Fixed assets (net) 31 Dec. 19 × 3	3362
New assets purchases planned (in cash budget but not in operating budget)	600
	3962
Less:	
Provision for depreciation during the year (in operating budget but not in cash budget) 330 + 34 + 24	388
Fixed assets (net) 31 Dec. 19 × 4	3574

Management is now in a position to complete its critical review of the plans for the year. On the basis of the total budgeted activites for the year the following values would emerge:

	Budget year 4
ROCE	5·62%
Margin on sales	3·81%
Turnover of capital employed	1·47 times
ROE	6·35%
Turnover of stock	3·27 times
Debtor collection period	58 days
Current ratio	1·3:1
Quick ratio	0·52:1

These values can be compared with those for the previous years which were calculated in chapter 7. Management must decide whether the deterioration in the major profitability and liquidity ratios is acceptable in the light of the environmental influences during the budget year.

12.

Use of financial data in decision taking

The commercial success of the company depends to a very large extent upon the capacity of top management to develop the appropriate strategies in a number of fields which conform to the general requirements of the long-term plans. The areas to be covered include:
—Strategies concerned with volume and capacity.
—Strategies for assessing the relative profitability of products or services.
—Strategies for pricing in conditions of spare capacity.
—Strategies for the direction of marketing effort.
—Strategies for selecting product range where there are capacity or other constraints.
The development of such strategies should be founded upon a proper understanding of the economics of each situation and the appropriate measure of cost.

Using the right data in the right way for each decision is of crucial importance for good decision making. Unfortunately, there is often confusion as to which data should be used. This confusion usually arises because systems have been developed and implemented for the collection and analysis of data and reporting results, such as budgetary control systems and product costing systems, and there is a great temptation to use the same data for reaching the decision. This could be quite wrong. Budgetary control systems and product cost systems have been prepared for quite specific purposes related to exercising the proper *control* of activities. They are based upon an analysis of all the data for a period and reporting on it in a way that is meaningful for managerial control. Decisions, on the other hand, must be based upon an analysis of *what costs would change* if one course of action is adopted rather than another. This requires first of all the ability to identify costs which are likely to vary within the context of the problem being considered, and then to decide how those changes are to be measured. One must also recognize that there are non-quantifiable factors related to some problems, such as the impact a particular decision may have upon labour relations or relations with the community. Such factors cannot be left out of the decision-making process. Indeed, in some cases they may more than outweigh the purely financial consequences. Finally, it should be recognized that where a decision involves a change in the amount of capital employed in the business, the change in the amount of profit cannot be the sole criterion for the decision. It must be related to the required change in investment in a capital investment appraisal decision.

Good methodology is also essential for good decision taking. All too often problem solving is completely unstructured and this can only lead to woolly decisions being taken. Indeed, very often the problem that one is trying to solve has itself not been clearly defined. The essential steps in the decision-making process are:

1. Clearly define the problem for which a solution is sought.
2. Set out all the possible alternative courses of action which could lead to a solution.
3. Discard those alternatives which on a commonsense appraisal are 'non-starters' for one reason or another.
4. Evaluate the cost and, where appropriate, the investment differences between each of the remaining courses of action.
5. Weigh up the non-quantifiable factors related to each course of action.
6. Taking into account the outcome of 4 and 5, reach a decision.

This chapter is concerned with those aspects of each decision which can be quantified, but directors and others must be prepared to identify and evaluate the non-quantifiable aspects if rational decision taking is to occur.

Cost/volume/profit relationships

One of the first aspects of costs that must be considered is their variability. Some costs, such as depreciation, rent and rates, are not affected by changes in the volume of activity. They are effectively fixed, whatever the level of output may be. Other costs may change more or less in proportion to changes in the output or provision of services. For example, the direct costs of producing products, the consumption of power, sales related commissions, etc., tend to move proportionately with output. The unit cost of producing a product or providing a service or activity is not a constant value but varies with the quantity of product produced or service provided, etc.

The manner in which costs vary with volume and the effect that this can have upon profits is perhaps best illustrated by means of a breakeven chart. It must be emphasized, however, that this technique can only be used to illustrate the economic relationships within an existing or proposed capacity. One cannot consider volumes in excess of that capacity since costs which have been fixed up to that point may then change considerably. For example, it would be necessary to acquire additional buildings and plant and equipment,

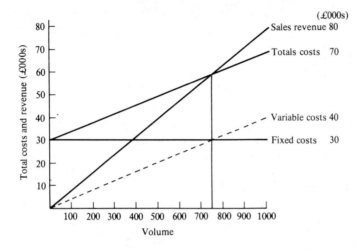

FIG. 12.1
The breakeven chart

extend managerial services, etc., all of which would increase the level of fixed costs.

The construction of a breakeven chart is illustrated in Fig. 12.1. It is based upon a company producing 'blips' which it sells for £80 each. It has a capacity to produce 1000 blips per month, and the fixed costs of that capacity are £30 000 per month. The variable production costs are £40 each.

The breakeven chart shows along the horizontal axis the volume of output and on the vertical axis the total costs and revenue. The scale of values on the horizontal axis cannot exceed the capacity and the limit to the values on the vertical scale is usually the total sales value that would be achieved at full capacity.

The fixed costs of £30 000 are represented on the chart by a horizontal straight line since fixed costs will remain the same irrespective of the volume of production. The total variable costs depend upon the level of activity and will range from zero, if nothing is produced, to £40 000, if 1000 units are produced. The total costs at each level of output is the aggregate of the fixed and variable cost for that volume. In practice the variable cost curve is not drawn on the chart, the total costs being drawn by simply adding the variable costs on top of the fixed costs.

The total revenue from sales also moves from zero value, if no products are sold, to £80 000, if the full 1000 blips are sold each month. The point at which total costs and total revenue are equal is the breakeven point, i.e., at the volume at which this occurs the company makes neither a profit nor a loss. In the case illustrated, the volume at which this occurs is 750 units of blips. The profit that would be earned or the loss incurred at other levels of output can be read off by measuring the gap between the total cost and total revenue for the appropriate volume.

The breakeven chart is a useful picture of the company as it is. It can also contribute to the analysis of the effect of different courses of action in the decision-making process. Let us assume, for example, that the problem requiring solution is too low a level of profitability. Proposals for rectifying this can be illustrated in the breakeven chart. For example, one of the courses of action in this case is to raise prices. This has the effect of raising the slope of the total revenue curve, thus increasing the gap between total costs and total revenue. Another proposal might be to reduce variable unit costs. This would have the effect of reducing the slope of the total cost curve. Both proposals would produce higher profits (or lower losses) the effect of the change being proportionately higher for higher volumes. One effect of the changes would be to reduce the breakeven point, the impact of which must be considered in this type of decision.

Assumptions on which breakeven charts are based

The type of breakeven chart used in the above illustration is based upon a number of assumptions which must be tested in the decision-making process. There is, first, the assumption that variable costs and product revenue change in a linear fashion, i.e., that unit variable cost and unit revenue remain constant values. This might not be the case. Pushing volume up towards capacity might move costs adversely, e.g., one might have to offer higher wages to attract the required staff or it might push up material prices. At the same time, the attempt to sell more products might move prices adversely through offering higher quantity discounts, etc. Such factors would need to be identified and built into the revenue and cost curves. Where a range of products is produced, the breakeven chart is based upon the assumption that the particular product mix which has been adopted for its construction will not change. If the products have quite different balances between unit revenue and unit variable costs then movements in the product mix will affect profit or loss.

Fixed costs themselves may not be entirely fixed. Some expenses which are treated as fixed costs (for example, management salaries) may change as the company moves nearer to capacity output, as it may be necessary to engage additional managerial staff to maintain the volume throughput. Nevertheless, if these limitations to the picture presented by the breakeven chart are carefully borne in mind it can be of considerable use to management in reaching decisions.

Contribution

The difference between the unit variable cost and the unit selling price in the previous example is called 'contribution', i.e., it is the amount which each unit produced contributes towards the fixed costs and profit of the business. The contribution achieved goes first towards covering the fixed costs, and when this happens all further contribution adds directly to profit. The volume at which it will start contributing to profit is the breakeven volume. If we refer to the data used in the previous example, the contribution is £40 per unit (selling price £80 minus £40 variable costs). When the output reaches 750 units the total contribution exactly matches the total fixed costs of £30 000. Beyond that volume the contribution per unit produced adds directly to profit at the rate of £40 for every extra unit produced.

Breakeven volume can therefore be ascertained mathematically using the following formula:

$$\text{Breakeven volume} = \frac{\text{Fixed costs}}{\text{Unit selling price} - \text{unit variable cost}}$$

This concept of contribution can be invaluable in many decision-making situations and can sometimes add to the clarity of some of the control processes. Since fixed costs are by definition fixed, and therefore will not differ whichever course of action is decided upon, the alternative course of action which maximizes contribution will automatically maximize profit. In other words, in the process of financial evaluation of the various courses of action fixed costs can be ignored. They are common to all the alternatives being considered and will not affect the issue. A further useful facet of contribution is that it enables one to avoid the sometimes arbitrary process of allocating fixed costs to products and saddling managers with costs which they are in no position to control.

The ways in which contribution can be used are illustrated in a series of problem situations in this chapter.

Capacity expansion

Expansion of capacity is a particularly critical decision as the wrong decision can lead to the company being saddled with additional fixed costs which the volume of output cannot cover. The breakeven analysis approach is particularly useful for illustrating the potential dangers of this decision. Let us assume that the company illustrated in the previous example was considering an expansion of capacity to 2000 units per month, and possibly to 3000 units. Each extra 1000 units of capacity would raise fixed costs by £30 000 per month and variable costs and selling price would remain the same.

The problem is shown in Fig. 12.2. The breakeven chart for the 1000 units per month has been extended to show a potential volume of 3000 units. The total cost curve up to the 1000 unit capacity is the same as that shown in Fig. 12.1. At point A_1 the total cost curve is increased by the additional £30 000 fixed costs to point A_2. From point A_2 to A_3 the slope of the curve

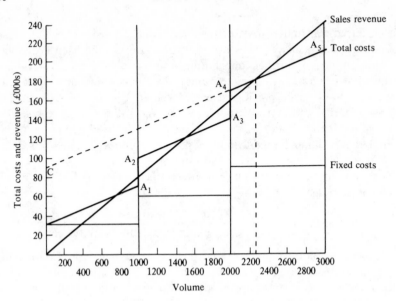

FIG. 12.2

Use of breakeven analysis in capacity expansion

is exactly the same as for volumes up to 1000 units i.e., it increases at the rate of £40 for every extra unit produced. The same thing happens when the capacity is raised to 3000 units. As the company moves from its existing capacity to 3000 units capacity the total cost curve for the business follows the line $A_1 \ldots \ldots A_5$. The total revenue is simply a linear extension of that shown in Fig. 12.1 rising to a total potential revenue at 3000 units per month of £240 000. As can be seen, there are potential areas of profit and loss in each capacity bracket with the area of possible profitability increasing as capacity is expanded.

The crucial factor in this decision, however, is that while the total cost curve goes up in the manner described as capacity is expanded, one cannot come down the same curve if volume contracts. If, for example, capacity is expanded to 3000 units per month the total cost curve now becomes C, A_4, A_5 and has a single breakeven of 2250 units per month. If management has miscalculated the potential increase in demand or some unanticipated event takes place which cuts demand, such as the oil price increase and its effect on motor manufacturers, then the future of the business may be at risk. In the example illustrated, if the company had kept to its original size of 1000 units capacity it could continue to make a profit at any volume in excess of

750. If it has gone on to a 3000 units per month capacity there is no way in which it can make a profit on a sales volume of less than 2250 per month.

The manufacturing unit as such may continue, but the present owners of the business are likely to lose all or most of their investment. Unless the board are able to sell off the surplus capacity or to fill it with other products the company will gradually slide into liquidation. All or some of the reconstituted production capacity may be acquired by other parties at a cost that enables them to make a profit.

The pricing decision

Many companies base their pricing policy on a build-up of total product or service cost and then add to this a percentage mark-up to cover any unallocated costs and profit. There are potential dangers in using this method of pricing which should be appreciated. Consider the following example. A company's budgeted costs for the year are:

	£	
Direct labour	30 000	(representing 20 000 hours of work)
Direct materials	20 000	
Overheads	90 000	

The budget is based upon using 15 000 hours of machine time during the year.
The company is asked to quote for a job the direct costs of which are:

	£
Direct labour	30 (40 hours of work)
Direct materials	80

The job would absorb 40 machine hours capacity.

What is 'the cost' of producing this job? Table 12.1 shows 'the cost' using four different overhead recovery rates and the price in each case is based upon adding a 20 per cent mark-up to 'the cost'. As can be seen from the results, the price quoted would vary considerably according to which overhead recovery method was adopted. Why should they be so different? The reason is that the cost 'mix' for this product differs considerably from the cost 'mix' for the business as a whole. For example, the ratio of labour to material costs for the business as a whole is 30:20 but for the job being quoted for it is 30:80. It is this kind of divergence which has produced the variety of measures of 'the cost'. If the whole range of products manufactured has the same cost 'mix' as the company as a whole the particular overhead recovery method will have little effect. But the more that mix starts to diverge from the mix for the company as a whole the more this problem will be encountered.

The problem in using this method of pricing can best be considered in a

TABLE 12.1
Pricing using different overhead recovery methods

	Percentage of direct labour cost	Percentage of direct materials	Rate per labour hour	Rate per machine hour
Overhead recovery rate:	300%	450%	£4·5 per hour	£6 per hour
	£	£	£	£
Direct labour	30	30	30	30
Direct materials	80	80	80	80
Overheads	90	360	180	240
'The cost'	200	470	290	350
20 per cent Mark-up	40	94	58	70
Price quoted	240	564	348	420

situation where the company quoting above is in competition with three other companies across broadly the same range of products. Let us assume that each of the four companies adopts a different method of overhead recovery. Each of the companies is relatively over-recovering overheads on some products and under-recovering them on others, although overall all overheads are recovered. The company that would be awarded the job in the above example is likely to be the one that is using the percentage of direct labour costs as the basis for recovering overheads. The long-term problem in this situation, if it is not detected, is that companies will tend to obtain work on products which have been undercharged with overheads, thus leading to low industry profitability.

The total cost and mark-up method of pricing is unrealistic in that in many cases price is fixed by competitive forces or what the market will bear. What directors should be concerned with is developing a system of measuring cost so that when that cost is compared with the market price they can decide:
1. Whether or not to withdraw from the market.
2. What products are more profitable than others.
What level of costs is relevant to this measurement? Consider the opposite two products. On a total cost basis the profit percentage is the same for both products and therefore management should be indifferent between the two. Would it be true, however, that if either of the products achieved an extra sales volume of £10 000 that in both cases the net profit would increase by £2000? No! The overheads include an element of fixed costs which would not change if the sales volume of either or both of the products were to change.

A more valid measurement of cost is the total variable cost basis used in the breakeven analysis. This tells us by how much costs change if one unit more or less of a product is made and sold. If we apply this basis to the two

	Product A £	Product B £
Direct materials	2	4
Direct labour	2	4
Overheads	4	8
Total cost	8	16
Net profit	2	4
Selling price	10	20
Profit/sales ratio	20%	20%

products the figures might look like those shown below. Measuring the relative profitability in this way tells us that Product B is more desirable than Product A. If £1000 extra sales of A are made it will add £300 to profit whereas the same extra sales of B would increase profit by £400.

	Product A £	Product B £
Direct materials	2	4
Direct labour	2	4
Variable overheads	3	4
Total variable cost	7	12
Contribution	3	8
Selling price	10	20
Contribution/sales ratio (CSR)	30%	40%

This measurement of profitability can contribute to product planning in a company, to decisions on how the scarce marketing resources are to be deployed, to assessing the relative profitability of different marketing channels, types of customer, and similar decisions. For example, if a company sold only the two products analysed above it would be advisable to switch most, if not all, of its marketing effort to promoting Product B, even if this means that some sales of A will be lost. After all, if £1000 sales of A are lost but a similar amount gained for B, profit is increased by £100, the difference between the contribution lost and that gained.

The contribution measurement can also form the basis of decisions in other fields. For example, in retailing the contribution made by products may be in terms of the contribution that they generate per square metre of shelf space occupied. Management may also have to consider whether to sell at prices lower than full cost and under what conditions. Again, the measure of contribution can be used.

Strategy for pricing where there is spare capacity

In some marketing situations it may be possible to segment the market in such a way that the bulk of the company's products can be sold in one or more segments at 'normal prices', i.e., prices which exceed the total cost, while the remainder of the company's output is sold in other market segments at prices in excess of variable cost only. Complete market segmentation is, of course, essential for the company to be able to do this, otherwise the sales at sub-normal prices may begin to affect the pricing in the main markets at full price.

In other marketing situations individual quotations may have to be given for each order taken. The problem in this market situation is to charge the maximum that the market will bear for each sale and at the same time to gain the maximum volume of business. If the company insists that all quotations must cover full cost plus a mark-up, business which cannot bear that price will be lost together with the contribution towards fixed costs and profit which it might have made. Any business obtained at a price greater than the variable costs of production and/or sales will add to profit, but that business will only be obtained if management has the foresight to realize the situation and price in a way which will maximize its chances of obtaining such orders.

Many managements would quite rightly be reluctant to place in the hands of their salesmen the freedom to quote prices at any figure above variable cost since there would be a tendency for all business to be quoted for on that basis and it is still true that a profit cannot be made until total costs have been covered. Directors should only sanction such a policy if they are quite sure that adequate safeguards have been built into the system. The safeguards comprise two elements: setting a minimum *average* contribution/sales ratio that must be achieved, and monitoring the actual contribution/sales ratio achieved continuously.

Setting the contribution/sales ratio

The overall contribution margin that is required can be directly related to the profitability targets set in the planning/budgeting process. For example, if the board have set a target ROCE of 15 per cent and have budgeted the fixed costs, sales, and capital employed for the period, the required contribution/sales ratio can be computed as shown below. As long as the 20 per cent

ROCE required: 15 per cent.
Budgeted capital employed: £1m.
Budgeted fixed costs: £450 000.
Budgeted sales: £3m.

Total contribution required   £
   Profit: 15 per cent of £1m.   =   150 000
   Fixed costs   =   450 000

                                600 000

Required contribution/sales ratio

$$\frac{600\,000 \times 100}{3m.} \quad = \quad 20 \text{ per cent}$$

contribution sales ratio is achieved, sales reach the £3 million budget, and spending on fixed costs does not exceed the budget, then the profit required to give the ROCE of 15 per cent will be earned. If, in the event, the sales budget cannot be achieved, the board has two choices. The contribution/sales ratio target can be maintained and a lower volume of sales accepted with the consequential adjustments that must be made to production budgets. Or the contribution/sales ratio can be lowered in order to try and maintain volume and take the strain of reduced sales potential on profit margins. In either case the potential effect on the ROCE can be calculated using a range of potential sales values and contribution/sales ratios.

Monitoring the contribution/sales ratio

The directors should then see that there is a manager directly charged with the task of ensuring that the target contribution/sales ratio is achieved. Reports should be regularly made to that manager on the sales volume per day or week or whatever period is most appropriate. Such reports should be based upon a register of sales orders taken in each period and the amount of contribution per order. In most businesses this imposes no additional work since a sales register is usually maintained and frequently includes the estimated profit for each order. This would need to be amended to include the contribution per order instead.

Direction of marketing effort

The effective use of marketing resources can make a significant contribution to a company's performance—indeed a critical one in some types of business. The resources devoted to marketing are not limitless and it is essential that they be used to the best effect. The director's role in relation to marketing can be summed up as follows:

1. He must decide what proportion of the firm's resources are to be allocated to the marketing function.
2. He must decide what marketing techniques and methods are to be used.
3. He must decide how the marketing effort as a whole is to be deployed.

It is with this latter function that this section is concerned.

The formulation of a policy for directing marketing effort should be based upon the identification of products or services which merit the maximum marketing resources being devoted to them and those which least merit the use of this scarce resource. In other words, products should be ranked in order of desirability on the criterion of relative profitability. The allocation decision can then be based upon this ranking and take into account any non-quantifiable factors, such as the need to continue to sell and promote the full range of products long term and other marketing constraints.

Since the effect of moving marketing resources from one product to another is likely to be a reduction in sales volume of one product and an increase in another, the measure of profitability to be used is once more based upon the way the revenue and costs of each of the products move as volume changes. i.e., on the contribution per unit of each of the products. In conditions where sales volume is the only constraint the relative ranking of products should be based upon the contribution/sales ratio.

Consider the data for Company Y given below. If the relative profitability of the four products (or services) is based upon the difference between the total cost and selling price then marketing effort should be concentrated upon products B and D, since on that criterion they are the only two products

Company Y

	Product A	Product B	Product C	Product D	Total
Selling price (£)	36	17	58	75	
Total cost (£)	38	15	59	72	
Variable cost (£)	22	12	30	65	
Net profit (loss) per unit (£)	(2)	2	(1)	3	
No. of units sold per year	20 000	30 000	3000	10 000	
Total sales value per year (£)	720 000	510 000	174 000	750 000	2 154 000
Total cost per year (£)	760 000	450 000	177 000	720 000	2 107 000
Total profit (loss) per year (£)	(40 000)	60 000	(3 000)	30 000	47 000
Fixed cost total (£)	567 000				

which are making a profit. What needs to be known in order to make the right decision, however, is by how much the costs and revenue of each product or service would change if one unit more or less of each of the products is sold as a result of redirecting the marketing effort, i.e., the measure of contribution. If relative profitability is measured in this way, as shown below, then it can be seen that product C is the most desirable product, followed by product A, and the marketing resources should be concentrated on these two products or services as far as other constraints may allow.

Company Y

	Product A	Product B	Product C	Product D	Total
Contribution per unit (£)	14	5	28	10	
Total contribution on last year's sales (£)	280 000	150 000	84 000	100 000	614 000
Contribution/sales ratio (%)	39	29	48	13	
			Less: Fixed costs (£)		567 000
			Net profit (£)		47 000

The effect on profit of a policy decision to devote most of the marketing effort to products C and A can be seen in the values shown below. This assumes that the redirection of the marketing effort moves some of the sales away from products B and D to products A and C, keeping within the total sales value of previous years. As can be seen, if the volume sold of each of the products is changed to those shown the net profit is increased from the present £47 000 to £205 000 although the total sales value is almost unchanged.

Company Y

	Product A	Product B	Product C	Product D	Total
No. sold	30 000	10 000	9 000	5 000	
Total sales value (£)	1 080 000	170 000	522 000	375 000	2 147 000
Total contribution (£)	420 000	50 000	252 000	50 000	772 000
			Less: Fixed costs (£)		567 000
			Net profit (£)		205 000

Other decisions in the marketing area can be made on the basis of contribution to sales ratio. For example, the relative merits of selling through different distribution channels, or of selling in different geographical areas can be based upon the relative contribution/sales ratio that can be achieved through each distribution channel or in each geographical area. One point must be stressed, however. That is that the decision bases discussed so far have all assumed that the sole factor limiting the company's total sales is its ability to sell, i.e., there are no constraints, such as limited production capacity, which impose limits on the level of activity. Where such conditions do exist, contribution will still be the basis for the decision, but instead of being related to sales it must be related to the units of the constraint.

Strategy where there are production or other constraints on volume

Where there are production or other constraints the objective of management should be to secure the greatest contribution possible for each unit of the constraint used. The desirability of selling products should be ranked by the contribution that each unit of product or service makes for each unit of the scarce resource that it uses. For example, if output is limited because there are only a limited number of machine hours available, management has to decide which products should be sold and which not sold. The optimum product mix would be the one where the available machine hours are filled with those products which produce the highest contribution for each hour of the machine time that it uses.

In practice it may not be possible to achieve the optimum product mix, nor is it necessarily desirable to do so. This is another situation where the non-quantifiable factors must receive consideration. In this situation there may be a number of marketing factors to take into account, e.g., the need to sell all the products in the long term, or the necessity of offering customers the complete product range to maintain market credibility. While such considerations must play their part in making a decision in this situation an essential part of that decision is to ascertain the optimum product mix so that the cost of deviating from that mix to meet other objectives is known.

Computing the optimum product mix

To illustrate the use of contribution in this context, assume a situation where a company has a power press capacity of only 10 000 hours per month which can be used on any of the company's products, and that it is not possible to increase that capacity in the immediate future. The potential sales for its products requires a number of press hours in excess of 10 000. The data for each of the products are given opposite.

If there was no capacity limitation the ranking of the products would be based on the contribution/sales ratio. On that basis D would be the most desirable product and C the least desirable. However, given the capacity limitation, the unit contribution must be divided by the number of hours required to produce one unit of each of the products. This produces the contribution for each hour of press time taken up by each product. For example, product A provides a contribution of £7·2 per unit, but takes up 2 hours of press time. It therefore provides a contribution of £3·6 for every hour of press time occupied. The ranking of products is based upon the relative contributions per press hour. On that basis the most desirable product is C and the least desirable D.

Having ranked the relative desirability of each product the optimum

Pro-duct	Total cost	Vari-able cost	Selling price	Contri-bution	CSR	No. of machine hours per units	Contri-bution per machine hour	Rank-ing	Poten-tial demand per month
				per unit					
	£	£	£	£	%		£		units
A	56·0	50·8	58·0	7·2	12·4	2·0	3·6	2	900
B	19·0	14·0	20·0	6·0	30·0	3·0	2·0	4	1500
C	51·5	47·6	54·0	6·4	11·9	1·6	4·0	1	800
D	8·4	7·0	10·6	3·6	34·0	2·0	1·8	5	1000
E	35·0	30·0	40·0	10·0	25·0	4·0	2·5	3	1200

Fixed costs are £20 000 per month

product mix can now be determined by filling the available press hours in descending order of desirability. This would produce the product mix and profit shown below. The product mix shown is the optimum mix and

Product	No. of units	Hours per unit	Total hours required	Contribution per unit	Total contribution
				£	£
C	800	1·6	1 280	6·4	5 120
A	900	2·0	1 800	7·2	6 480
E	1 200	4·0	4 800	10·0	12 000
B	706	3·0	2 118	6·0	4 236
			9 998		27 836
				Less: Fixed cost	20 000
				Profit	7 836

the profit for that mix can be computed by multiplying the unit contribution for the products to be made by the numbers produced and from the total contribution from products included in the mix to deduct the total fixed cost. The profit cannot be increased by substituting some product not in the mix for those included since the products so substituted would earn a lower contribution for the press hours that they would absorb than those products that they would be displacing.

An important point to note in the above example is that the ranking of products on a contribution/sales ratio was quite different from that which emerged when the contribution per press hour was used. It is essential that the right measure should be used for the circumstances in which the company finds itself, and that if the company moves from a state of production or other constraint to one where the ability to sell is the sole limiting factor, or vice versa, this fact is known and the ranking of products is reappraised so that a new strategy can be formulated.

Where there are two or more simultaneous constraints the problem is more difficult to resolve. Techniques such as linear programming can be used to compute the optimum product mix in such circumstances.

The approach that has been adopted above in determining the optimum product mix can be used in any situation where there is a major factor which is in limited supply and is crucial for the success of the company. For example, shelf or display space is a major factor in retailing and the best utilization of the space can be decided on the basis of the relative contribution each product makes for each square metre of display used.

Unprofitable product lines

It follows from the discussion on contribution that decisions to add to or delete product lines should not be made on the criterion of whether or not that product makes a profit after taking into account total cost. As long as a product or service produces a greater revenue than the additional costs it would incur it is best to retain that product line since it makes a contribution to fixed costs and therefore relieves the burden of fixed costs on other products to the extent of the excess of the additional revenue over the additional costs. Only if it is possible to utilize the resources that the product uses for a more profitable product should its deletion from the product range be considered.

Ad hoc decisions

So far the problems discussed have been resolved on the basis of the division of costs between those that are fixed and those that are variable within the constraint of an existing capacity. They properly fall within the application of what is frequently called marginal costing, i.e., measuring by how much costs and revenue change if one additional unit of a product is produced. Other decisions may have to be based upon the cost differences between different courses of action, or what should preferably be called 'differential costing'. In a situation where a choice has to be made between several courses of action, what must be identified is the amount by which costs will change if one course of action is taken rather than another. The principal difficulty in this situation is to identify which costs would change and by how much.

A typical problem in this area is the 'make or buy' decision. Management has to make a choice between buying a component or part from an outside manufacturer or making it within the company. The cost differences to identify, therefore, are those which are incurred if the company buys in the parts and the additional costs that it would incur if it makes the products itself. This is illustrated in the following example.

Assume that a company currently purchases its total annual requirement of 10 000 units of a sub-assembly K123 at a cost of £2 per unit. The production manager proposes that the company should now make this sub-assembly. There is adequate space within the company to do so and the cost accountant has provided cost data for the item as follows:

> Direct materials   60p per unit
> Direct labour   70p per unit
> The overhead rate for the department
> that would carry out manufacture is 200
> per cent of direct labour cost.

An investigation has been made of the additional overheads that would be incurred and this shows the following:

	£
Supervision	2500
Power	800
Depreciation	500
Other expenses	1300
	5100

The costs incurred under each alternative which would not be incurred if the other alternative is adopted can be set out as follows:

Buying from outside		Own manufacture	
	£		£
10 000 units @ £2 each	20 000	Materials 10 000 × 60 p	6 000
		Labour 10 000 × 70p	7 000
		Overheads	5 100
			18 100

It appears from the above comparison that the company could increase its profit by £1900 if it makes the sub-assembly itself. Note that the departmental overhead rate is not relevant to this decision. It is the amount by which overheads will actually *change* that is relevant for this decision. The overhead rate is a measurement used for *control* purposes, not for decision making. If management decides to manufacture rather than to buy, then the total overhead for the department will be spread over the extended range of production and should be reduced, so that for control purposes the existing products bear a lower proportion of the overheads as some of them are now allocated to the new production.

While the above analysis sets out the financial criteria for the decision, once more non-financial criteria may be important. For example, filling spare capacity with such work reduces the flexibility of the business to respond to any upsurge in work at normal prices. Design changes may be effected more easily if the whole of the production is 'in house', and so on.

The make or buy decision set out above illustrates a further aspect which must be taken into account in many decisions. One of the additional overhead expenses was depreciation. This implies that there would be a requirement for additional investment in fixed assets. The simple effect of change in profit is not in this case an adequate test. What should happen when the amount of additional profit has been determined is to test this against the additional investment required in a capital investment appraisal decision to ascertain the rate of return that would be earned on the investment. It is this rate that provides the final solution to this problem. In any situation where the solution of a problem involves additional investment of capital, whether in fixed assets or current assets, the final decision should only be made on the basis of the results of the capital investment appraisal.

13.
Planning and appraising long-term investment

The planning and appraisal of new investment in a company is a function which properly belongs to the directors. They have the duty of deciding what criteria are to be applied in identifying and selecting investment opportunities and of establishing an organizational framework within which capital investment decisions are made. If directors do not exercise this function resources are likely to be allocated to uses in a haphazard fortuitous manner, with no effective appraisal of the various investment opportunities. In some cases, of course, managerial 'hunch' works, but the more complex the company, the more sophisticated its activities, the less likely is this to be the case.

In its importance for the long-term viability and liquidity of the company the capital investment decision ranks second only to long-term planning. They are critical decisions about how the funds available to the company are to be deployed in terms of assets and activities. Individual decisions can involve substantial proportions of the company's funds and their success or failure can have a significant impact upon the company as a whole. It is right, therefore, that much of senior management's time and effort should be directed to this area. There are three essential ingredients for the successful development of the company:
1. Identifying the right ideas and opportunities.
2. Selecting the right 'package' of investments.
3. Effective management of the projects selected.

Identifying opportunities
Identifying opportunities for investment is at the very heart of a successful business, whether those opportunities arise from the company's research and development activities or from changes in the environment or from the use of new technologies. In the small to medium-sized company the directors may be actively involved in or be aware of trends that may affect their company. In the larger business this direct involvement may not be possible in all areas, in which case the directors should ensure that the organizational

framework provides the maximum possibility that opportunities which may benefit the company are quickly identified and acted upon. This aspect was dealt with on p. 96.

In their appraisal of projects placed before them for approval directors should exercise their critical faculties. The detailed calculations of the project will have been carried out by others. The directors' function is to test the assumptions on which the project has been based and to ensure that all alternative ways of achieving the purpose of the project have been examined. All too often only one method of achieving the objective of the project is considered whereas there may be other ways that would be more advantageous to the company.

Selecting projects

From the variety of investment projects available the board must select those which most help the long-term growth and profitability of the company. Within the framework of the long-term plans this means that, in general, the selection is made from available opportunities on the criterion of profitability. The usual situation is that the company has a limited amount of capital for investment and this should be used to finance higher yielding projects rather than lower yielding ones, subject to certain overall constraints that are discussed later.

Even if a company had unlimited access to capital, that capital has a cost, whether of interest (in the case of loans), or the return the shareholders could have earned if their funds were invested elsewhere (in the case of share-holders' funds). It would be wrong to invest funds in projects which would earn less than that cost. Individual project selection should therefore be made against two criteria:

1. Relative profitability.
2. A minimum acceptable rate of return which is greater than the cost of capital.

Overall criteria can then be applied to the batch of projects selected. The first is to ensure that the cash flows of the company, if that batch is approved, would not have periods of major cash deficiency. This might occur, for example, if the projects have several years of negative cash flows and the large positive flows all occur later in the life of the projects. In this situation it might be better to adopt a mix of projects which, while less profitable, provides a smoother pattern of cash flows.

The second criterion is the effect the projects would have on reported profits. Again, if the profits from the projects emerge only late in their life the reported earnings over the next few years might be reduced with adverse effects on the share price and the company's ability to raise new capital.

The directors' role

The directors have a duty to establish the financial criteria that are to be used in the selection process. They should be aware of the cost of capital to the company, which should be an absolute minimum rate of return. Preferably, however, the board should set a target rate of return based upon the profitability required to fulfil the long-term plans and this should be used as a cut-off rate below which projects will not be accepted. Any project appraisal system operating without such guidelines is operating in a managerial vacuum and is unlikely to be successful.

Effective management of projects

The potential benefit of good projects is lost if they are poorly managed when operational. Most of these problems are dealt with in the chapter on operational planning and control. At the appraisal stage, however, it might be possible to assist this process, particularly for major projects, by identifying the critical elements in the project which require the tightest control. This can be done by testing how sensitive the rate of return is to changes in the major elements of the project. If the rate of return is particularly sensitive to changes in certain factors then those factors should be investigated more rigorously before the project is approved. They are also the factors which require the strictest management control when operating and around which the reporting structure should be centred.

The control structure can be supplemented by a post-audit procedure after a project is operational to test the validity of the assumptions and forecasts on which the project was based and how effectively these are working out in practice.

Setting up the capital budgeting system

The capital budgeting system is made up of three principal elements.
1. Identifying and measuring the value of funds available for investment in the period.
2. Establishing the criteria to be used in deciding which projects should be approved.
3. The detailed preparation of projects and their submission for approval.
Both 1 and 2 should be the subject of board-level decisions harmonized with the long-term objectives and the need to maintain appropriate profitability and liquidity ratios period by period. In the case of 3, the system developed depends upon the size and nature of the business. The common elements are:
—Line management will be responsible, with the appropriate technical support, for the development and submission of detailed projects.
—There should be an independent appraisal of the assumptions on which projects are based and the return on investment calculations, at least as far as major projects are concerned.
—Approval for projects should be at the highest level.
—To ensure that projects coming forward for approval conform to the long-term requirements, line managers should be aware of those requirements.

Appraisal techniques

Since profitability is an essential element in the selection of investment projects the various techniques available should be tested to see how effectively they measure profitability.

Accounting rate of return

This method attempts to measure the average profit per year and to express this as a rate of return on a measure of the capital invested. For example, if the project has a four-year life, requires an investment of £10 000, and achieves yearly profits as shown for project A in Table 13.1, it has average annual

TABLE 13.1
The accounting rate of return

	Project A £	Project B £	Project C £
Investment	10 000	10 000	10 000
Annual profits:			
Year 1	4 000	1 000	2 500
Year 2	3 000	2 000	2 500
Year 3	2 000	3 000	2 500
Year 4	1 000	4 000	2 500
Year 5	—	—	2 500
Total profits	10 000	10 000	12 500
Average annual profit	2 500	2 500	2 500
Per cent return on investment	25%	25%	25%

profits of £2500. Expressed as a percentage of the original investment of £10 000 this represents a rate of return of 25 per cent. There are certain technical difficulties. Should profits be measured before or after tax? Should profits be expressed as a percentage of the original investment or the average investment over the life of the project? These problems could be overcome by adopting a common basis for all projects.

The real problem arises when it comes to making a choice between different projects. For example, if one had to choose between projects A and B in Table 13.1, the accounting rate of return shows that they are equally profitable and that one should be indifferent between the two. However, it can be readily seen that the profit flows from project B arise later than those for A and are therefore less valuable. Since money has a time value, A would be the better investment.

The choice between A and B was simple because the only difference between them was that the pattern of profit flows was reversed. How can one make a choice between project A and project C? The latter has higher total earnings over the life of the project but the same average earnings per year. How then can one relate the higher earnings of A in years 1 and 2 with the higher earnings of C in years 3, 4 and 5? Without some formal mathematical basis this is impossible.

The accounting rate of return method is therefore inefficient in measuring profitability in that it does not take into account the differences in the timing of profits or in their duration.

The pay-back period

As its name suggests, this method is based upon measuring the length of time a project takes to recoup the capital invested in it. Since capital cannot be said to be recouped until cash has been received this method is usually based upon cash flows rather than profits. For this purpose cash flows can be defined as profit plus depreciation. For example, project A in Table 13.2 has a three-year life and the cash flows shown give a pay-back period of three years, i.e., at the end of the third year the cumulative cash flows equal the investment. Project B in the same Table has a pay-back of $4\frac{1}{3}$ years. If this is used as the selection technique it would indicate that project A should be accepted rather than B.

This would be wrong, since project A has a rate of return of zero. Its cash receipts just match the cash invested. Project B has a positive rate of return

TABLE 13.2
The pay-back period

	Project A £	Project B £
Investment	10 000	10 000
Cash flows:		
Year 1	4 000	1 000
Year 2	3 000	2 000
Year 3	3 000	3 000
Year 4		3 000
		£3 000 p.a. for another 10 years
Pay-back period	3 years	$4\frac{1}{3}$ years

since the cash receipts are greater than the investment, although the rate of return has not been calculated.

Pay-back does not attempt to measure profitability since it takes no account of cash flows received after the pay-back period. However, it may be a useful initial screening device for projects in some cases, particularly where the time by which the investment has to be recouped is critical.

Discounted cash flow (DCF)

DCF techniques take into account the different timing of cash flows and differing lives of projects. They require no complex mathematical calculations, being simply the reciprocal of compound interest.

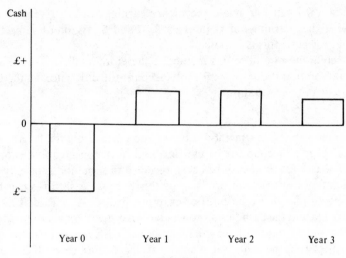

FIG. 13.1
Cash flow profile of an investment project

The cash flow profile for a simple project is shown in Fig. 13.1. There is an initial outflow of cash followed by a series of cash flows coming back from the project. The essential element of DCF is to value all the years' cash flows on a common time basis. Since the decisions are being made now it is usual to use the present time or the year of investment as the common time basis.

The DCF rate of return

In bringing the future cash flows back to their value at the present time a rate of discounting is used. The higher that rate of discounting the lower is the present value of those cash flows, and vice versa. By adjusting the rate of discounting it should be possible to find a discount rate which equates the present value of the cash flows with the amount of the investment. Or, looking at both inward and outward cash flows, they have a zero net present value. When this position is found the rate of discount is the rate of return on the project.

This method is illustrated in Fig. 13.2. The cash flows in years 1, 2, and 3 are discounted back to the present. By trial and error a rate of discounting is found which equates the present value of the inward cash flows with the investment.

The mathematics of discounting

There is nothing difficult about the mathematics of discounting. Line 1 of Table 13.3 shows how a sum of money grows over time using compound interest of 10 per cent. By the end of the second year £100 invested now would have grown to £121. Line 2 shows the discounting process. As can be seen,

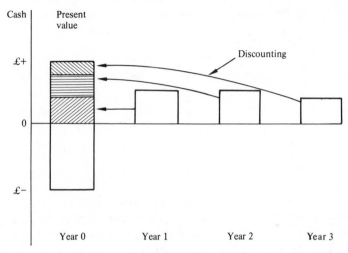

FIG. 13.2
The discounting process

the series of values are the same, the only difference is that discounting takes future values and brings them back to the present while compound interest takes present values and carries them into the future.

If £110 receivable in one year's time has a present value of £100, one can also say that £1 receivable in one year's time has a present value of 100/110 or £0·909 since £0·909 invested now would grow to £1 at the end of one year at an interest rate of 10 per cent. 0·909 is a present value factor and if tables of these are produced for different interest rates and different periods of time

TABLE 13.3
Compound interest and discounting

	Now	1 year	2 years
Compound interest at 10%	£100 ⟶	£110 ⟶	£121
Discounting at 10%	£100 ⟵	£110 ⟵	£121
Present value factors	$\dfrac{100}{121}$ ⟵	110	
	$\dfrac{110}{110}$		
	= 0·909		
	$\dfrac{100}{121}$ ⟵		121
	= 0·826		

they can be used for discounting, since to find the present value of a future sum of money it only has to be multiplied by the appropriate present value (PV) factor. There is nothing more than this to the mathematics of discounting.

The use of present value factors can be illustrated in a simple example. A project requires an investment of £200 and will result in cash flows in each of the following two years of £115. What is the rate of return on the project?

Investment £200

Year	Cash flow £	PV factor 8%	Present value £	PV factor 10%	Present value £
1	115	0·926	106·5	0·909	104·5
2	115	0·857	98·6	0·826	95·0
			205·1		199·5

The present value factors for 8 per cent have been tried first. These produce a total present value for the two years' cash flows of £205·1 which is greater than the investment of £200. The rate of 8 per cent is therefore too low and a higher rate must be tried. The factors for 10 per cent are now tried and the present value now comes to £199·5 which means that the rate of return on the project is almost 10 per cent and is near enough for practical purposes.

What does the DCF rate of return mean?

In the example just used, the DCF rate of return of 10 per cent means that if the cost of capital to the company is 10 per cent this project would just cover the cost of funds invested in it. Or, more explicitly, the cash flows are sufficient to repay the capital invested and provide a return of 10 per cent on the capital invested in the project in each year of its life.

This can be seen by using the same data in a more familiar situation— borrowing from a building society. A loan is made of £200, the building society charges 10 per cent interest on the amount of the loan outstanding at the beginning of each year. On this basis £115 would have to be paid to the building society in each of the two years as follows:

		£	£
Loan			200
Year 1:	Payments	115	
	Interest on £200	20	
	Repayment of loan		95

	£	£
Year 2: Loan outstanding at the beginning of year		105
Payments	115	
Interest on £105	10·5	
Repayment of loan		104·5
		0·5

As can be seen, the two years' repayments have been sufficient to repay the loan and to provide a return of 10 per cent on the amount outstanding at the beginning of each year. Each investment project in a company can be considered as borrowing a part of the capital employed and what the DCF rate of return expresses is the interest the project could afford to pay on the funds invested in each year, given the pattern of cash flows. In any project, once the rate of return has been found the cash flows can be broken down into their interest and capital repayment elements in the manner shown above.

Net present value, using DCF (NPV)

Instead of finding the actual rate of return this method involves applying a pre-determined minimum rate of return in the discounting process to ascertain whether the project meets that minimum rate. If the present value of the cash flows is greater than the investment (or the net present value of all cash flows is positive) then the project exceeds the minimum rate of return. If it is less (or the NPV is negative) then it does not meet the minimum rate.

This method has not so far provided the facility for ranking projects in order of profitability. This can be achieved by calculating the *profitability index*. For example, taking the values used in the previous project and assuming that the minimum rate of return is 8 per cent, the present value of the cash flows using that discount rate is £205·1 against an investment of £200. The project therefore has a rate of return higher than the minimum. The profitability index would be calculated by dividing the present value by the amount of the investment, i.e., 205·1/200·0 = 1·025. The acceptable projects can now be ranked on a profitability index.

The technique of discounting is quite straightforward and can be left to those concerned with submitting and vetting investment proposals, and in many ways it is the least important element in project preparation and evaluation. What is more important is what goes into the calculation of the cash flows. Directors should only be interested in the technique to the extent that they understand the end result of the appraisal process.

Make-up of the cash flows

More important for the director is the questioning of the assumptions on which the cash flows have been based. Are the sales volumes and prices and the elements of cost dealt with correctly? Are the cost savings expected to result from investing in more automated machines realistic? Is the expected cost of the investment supported by adequate evidence and has any planned change in working capital been included? It is sometimes forgotten that an increase in the working capital is just as much a capital investment as is new plant.

Equally important is to ensure that a full search has been made for all alternative ways of carrying out a project. Since most project proposals originate from line management there is an understandable tendency for the proposal to be framed in terms of maximum investment and maximum profit increase. However, this may not make the optimum use of the scarce resource of capital. A simpler form of the project with a lower investment, lower profit, but a higher rate of return may be better for the company.

Consider the example of a situation where there are two ways of carrying out the project. One requires an investment of £40 000 and would provide a rate of return of 15 per cent, the other requires an investment of only £20 000 and provides a return of 20 per cent. While the 15 per cent return on the former may be an acceptable rate of return, the fact is that the incremental investment of £20 000 to achieve the higher investment cost would provide a rate of return of only 10 per cent. This may not be an acceptable rate, and even if it was, the company may have plenty of other investment opportunities offering returns in excess of 10 per cent. The company should invest the incremental £20 000 in such uses rather than in the more sophisticated form of the project.

The most efficient use of capital should be the prime objective of the policies pursued by the board, together with the need to ensure that the mix of projects selected are acceptable in terms of their effect on the profit and cash flow pattern for the company as a whole and are conducive to the achievement of its long-term objectives.

Risk and uncertainty

Few if any projects are free of risk and many are subject to major areas of risk, both commercial and political. A new product launch is a typical example of the commercial uncertainties of the market and production cost risk. While it is simple to evaluate a project on the basis that £x of investment will increase profits by £y, one knows that in fact both x and y are the most probable values drawn from a range of possible values.

One way of dealing with this problem, particularly as far as major projects are concerned, is to obtain some estimate of the probability of the different rates of return that might be achieved (probability analysis). Another is to

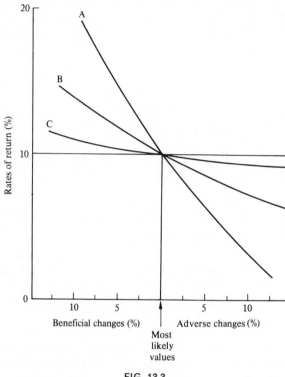

FIG. 13.3
Sensitivity analysis

explore the sensitivity of the rate of return to changes in individual elements of the project (sensitivity analysis).

Probability analysis

Standard computer packages are available for this purpose. They are based upon estimating ranges of values and probabilities for the elements of each project, such as sales volume, selling prices, groups of costs, amount of the investment. The program then proceeds to carry out a series of rate of return calculations by randomly selecting values from the range for each item. The number of times a particular value is used depends upon its probability. The outcome of the process is that a probability distribution of the likely rates of return is provided for the appropriate projects. If one project has a higher probability of exceeding a given rate of return than another then that project is more desirable.

Sensitivity analysis

The objective of sensitivity analysis is to answer the 'What if?' type of question that management should be asking—e.g., what happens to the rate of return if material costs turn out to be 10 per cent higher than those included in the data? The answers to such questions can be found by holding all the other data for the project constant and varying that factor which is being investigated.

Sensitivity analysis formalizes this process by investigating each significant element in the project independently and comparing the relative sensitivity of the rate of return to each factor considered. For example, the project illustrated in Fig. 13.3 has a predicted rate of return of 10 per cent. Beneficial and adverse changes in three elements of the project, A, B, and C, are explored and rates of return related to each change plotted in the form of a curve. In the example shown it can be seen that the rate of return is much more sensitive to changes in factor A than it is for the other factors.

This fact has managerial significance. Factor A can now be more thoroughly explored before the project is approved and the basis of the assumptions used tested. It identifies the areas where the most stringent management control is required. Management may also call for immediate reports if that factor in the event deviates by more than a given percentage from the values incorporated in the project—both to cut off the project if the change is adverse, or to reinforce what is likely to be a very successful project with more investment if the change is beneficial.

Inflation

Capital projects cover a number of years and a continuing worry for directors is whether inflation may completely invalidate the premises on which the selection of projects was made. The short answer is that if costs and revenue all inflate at the same rate inflation has no effect on the rate of return achieved, providing that the 100 per cent first year capital allowances continue. What can seriously affect the profitability of the project is:

1. When one or more elements in the costs of the project inflate at a different rate from the general rate of inflation.
2. If 1 happens, then how significant is the value of the costs involved in relation to the amount of the investment in the project?
3. Where there are obstacles to adjusting prices to cost inflation, such as long-term fixed-price contracts or government intervention. The longer the delay in the adjustment, the bigger the effect.

If any of these conditions prevail the elements of the cash flow must first be computed in pounds of each of the future years and when the total has been ascertained, each years' total pounds of that year must be converted to pounds of the present year and then discounted in the normal way.

Post audit

The overall control of capital budgeting is incomplete without some form of audit of projects once they are operational. This holds for a number of reasons. The most important is the discipline it imposes on those forecasting the values to be used in the project appraisal. The knowledge that these will be checked against the values actually achieved should lead to more care being taken in framing estimates, etc. Second, lessons can be learned from the post audit which can improve the forecasting of future projects. Last, it may be possible over time to distinguish between the optimistic manager and the pessimistic one so that this can be allowed for in the project evaluation. It cannot be emphasized too much that the quality of investment appraisal is dependent most of all on good planning and budgeting of projects, rather than the selection technique used.

General conclusions

Before approving the planned investments for the year the board must give close consideration to two factors already mentioned. What impact will that mix of projects have on the cash flows and the profit flows? These must be judged in the light of the company's overall performance and how investors may view the company. Adverse trends in either of these factors may have severe repercussions on the company by limiting the funds available for future investment.

14.
Combating inflation

No one should try to disguise the evil of inflation. Quite apart from the damage it can cause to the social fabric of a nation, it can wreak havoc on the measuring and controlling systems used in business. Above all, through the distortions it induces in company financial reports, particularly in the statement of values in the balance sheet and the measurement of profit in the profit and loss account, it can lead to the gradual liquidation of a company unless the dangers are clearly seen by the board.

The monetary unit

Financial accounting and reporting uses a common denominator—the national money unit. The activities of the business are recorded in terms of that money unit and it is used to express the outcome of those activities. In times of inflation, however, the underlying value of the measuring unit is itself changing—a 1976 pound is something quite different from a 1975 pound, let alone a 1955 pound. One can well imagine the consternation that would be caused if other units of measure such as the metre or litre were subject to the same variability. Yet the variability of the money unit can put the business entity itself at risk unless steps are taken to counter the effects of inflation in financial reporting and in decision taking.

What is profit?

It cannot really be said that a company has made a profit unless it has charged against its sales revenue for the period all costs incurred and maintains its capital intact in real terms. Consider a simple situation where a company simply buys and sells cans of beans and has no overhead expenses. At the beginning of the month it carries a stock of 1000 cans of beans that it had purchased at a price of 10p each. Its balance sheet at the beginning of the period would therefore appear as follows:

Balance sheet at beginning of period

	£		£
Capital	100	Stock of beans	100

During the month the beans are all sold for 11p each and the business purchases a further 1000 cans at a price of 12p each. Has the business made a profit and, if so, how much?

If the profit is measured on the normal basis of historic cost a profit of £10 has been made, since goods which had cost £100 have been sold for £110. However, consider the balance sheet as it would appear at the end of that period based upon £10 of reported profit.

Balance sheet at end of period

	£		£
Capital	100	Stock of beans	120
Profit	10		
Loan	10		
	120		120

The stock required to bring the business to the same physical state at which it started the period has cost it £120, and in order to pay for the stock the business has had to borrow £10. In other words, simply to stand still the company would have to borrow money, yet the historical accounts show it as earning a profit.

The reality of the situation is, of course, that the business has not made a profit at all in real terms, but rather it has made a loss of £10 and it is now having to borrow £10 to replace the capital it has lost in order to keep the business going. The plight of the business becomes even more grave when the 'profits' are taxed and some of them may be distributed to the owners of the business. It is a situation which, if repeated over a number of accounting periods, will quickly bring the business up against limits to its borrowing powers, and, unless corrected, to eventual liquidation.

The above example highlights the 'stock profit' element of company earnings in times of inflation. That is to say that some of the profits reported on a historical basis are due solely to holding stocks of goods whose value has increased due to the effect of changes in the purchasing power of the money unit. If companies are to guard against the 'doomsday effect' of the situation, the 'profits' arising from simply holding stocks must be distinguished from those arising from trading activities as measured in real terms. In the UK the tax problem has been partially solved by the provision of relief for increases in the value of stocks. Broadly, any increase in stock value between the beginning and end of the year less 15 per cent of the profit for the period is allowable as a charge against profit before computing the tax liability. This is only rough and ready justice since a company might not increase its value of stock because the physical quantity is reduced and it would therefore not gain from such relief.

The stock profit element is only one of the distorting factors. Further problems arise through the ownership of fixed assets. Consider the situation where a company purchased a machine in 1970 for £10 000 and is depreciating it straight-line over 10 years. The machine is replaced in 1980 by a similar machine which costs £20 000. On a historic cost basis the profits for each of the years during that 10-year period will have borne a depreciation charge of £1000 and the company has therefore retained £10 000 of its earnings to cover the replacement of the asset. The cost of the replacement is, however, £20 000. Where is the extra £10 000 to come from?

It will come, of course, from borrowing unless the board makes special provisions during the life of the asset to cover the eventual replacement. Just as with stock, the holding of fixed assets in times of inflation will result in the overstating of profits in real terms and those profits may be distributed as dividends. The tax effect is mitigated where 100 per cent first year allowances can be taken, since the tax relief and the cost are both measured in similar pounds.

This then is the 'doomsday machine' of inflation. If new methods of reporting profits are not devised then company reports will continue to a greater or lesser extent to overstate profits, and if those illusory profits are taxed and distributed, the company is consuming its real capital and increasingly financing its continued existence by debt.

The directors must consider the problem of inflation from two points of view:
1. How can the company's financial report be structured to show real profits separately from the effects of inflation?
2. How should management planning and control be modified so that decisions take into account the problem of inflation?

The financial report

Two attempts have been made to change financial reporting so that it reflects the impact of inflation and isolates changes due to inflation from those due to the trading activities of the business. The first of these is the provisional SSAP 7: 'Accounting for changes in the purchasing power of money'. The second is the Sandilands Report, which was published in September 1975 and which proposes a basis called *current cost accounting* (CCA). Neither is altogether satisfactory and it is quite possible that what finally will emerge is a combination of the best feature of each.

SSAP 7. Accounting for changes in the purchasing power of money

This statement represents the first step taken by the accounting profession to deal with the problem of distortions caused in financial reports by the effects of inflation. Currently (1976) it is only a provisional standard and is therefore not obligatory. The Sandilands Report rejected the philosophy incorporated into this standard. Eventually it will be superseded by a new standard that takes into account the Sandiland's Report which it is recommended should come into force in December 1977.

To fully appreciate the underlying philosophy of this statement it is necessary to distinguish between two different factors which cause changes in value. There are, first, those factors which cause relative changes in the costs of goods and services in different industries, movements which take place irrespective of inflation, e.g., the per ton cost of transporting oil due to the introduction of supertankers and the reduction in unit cost of many high technology products as they are brought to the stage of mass production. The statement is not concerned with such changes in value.

The second factor which causes changes in value is changes in the purchasing power of the monetary unit in which accounts are presented—in other words, periods of inflation or deflation. It is this aspect which is the concern of this standard. It is important that managers and other users of financial statements should understand the effect that changes in the purchasing power of the monetary unit can have on costs, profits, distribution policies, dividend cover, the exercise of borrowing powers, returns on funds, and future cash needs.

Inflation affects the balance sheet items in different ways. Items which are expressed in fixed money terms (called monetary items) have a constant value expressed in money terms but a declining value in real terms. This group includes debtors, cash, creditors and loans. Other items in the balance sheet represent physical assets, such as buildings, plant and equipment, and stock. These are non-monetary items and have a constant value in real terms (subject to the relative inter-industry adjustments already mentioned) but an increasing value in money terms. The equity interest of the shareholders is a claim on the net monetary and non-monetary assets and therefore falls into neither category.

The basis of the statements is that, while companies should continue to keep their records and present the financial reports as hitherto in terms of historic pounds, listed companies should present to the shareholders a supplementary statement which converts the items to their value in terms of pounds at the balance sheet date. The conversion of the historic pounds to current pounds in the supplementary statement is to be made on the basis of the general index of retail prices (or its predecessors), or in the Republic of Ireland the official consumer price index. Directors are responsible for the form of the presentation of the supplementary statement and should state in a note the basis on which it has been prepared.

The conversion process

There are four basic steps in the conversion process:

1. Items in the balance sheet at the beginning of the year are converted into pounds at their purchasing power at the beginning of the year on the following basis:
   (a) non-monetary items are adjusted for changes in purchasing power since they were acquired or revalued;
   (b) monetary items require no conversion, as they are in terms of current purchasing power at all times.
2. The values of *all* the items in the opening balance sheet are then updated from the current purchasing power (CPP) value at that date to their value at that date expressed in pounds of the purchasing value at the end of the year. This means that non-monetary items which have not changed during the year will be expressed at the same value at both the beginning and end of the year. On the other hand, monetary items that have not changed during the year will be shown at a higher value at the beginning of the year than at the end, the difference representing the decline in the real value of this item over the year.
3. Items in the balance sheet at the end of the year are converted into pounds of purchasing power at the end of the year on the same basis as used in 1.
4. The difference between the total equity interest in the converted balance sheets at the beginning and end of the year, after adjustment for dividends paid and the introduction of new capital, represents the profit or loss for the year expressed in pounds of purchasing power at the end of the year. This should be supported by a summarized profit and loss account in the same format as the conventional account in which sales are re-stated at their value in end-of-year pounds, the adjusted profit before tax, the tax charge (this will be the same value as shown in the historic account, since CPP accounting is not accepted by the Inland Revenue), the dividend, and the restated retained profits. Comparative figures for the previous year should be shown.

The difference between the profit before tax on a historic basis and that on a CPP basis for both the current and previous years should be explained and includes the items below.

Stock An additional charge representing the difference between the cost of the stock at the beginning of the year and its CPP value at that time in order to take out the inflation element in the profit recorded when that stock is sold.

Depreciation The additional depreciation that must be provided to take account of the increased money value of fixed assets.

Monetary items The net gain in purchasing power due to the reduction in the real value of net monetary liabilities.

Sales, purchases, and all other costs These are increased by the change in the index between the average date on which they occurred and the end of the year.

Last year's adjusted profit Last year's adjusted profit is stated in pounds of purchasing power at the end of that year. This must now be adjusted in total to pounds of equivalent purchasing power at the end of the current year so that both years' profits can be compared in pounds of the same purchasing power.

The supplementary statement need not deal with each item in the accounts individually but can be in a reasonably summarized form. It can be no more than an approximation and over-elaborate precision is unnecessary. The auditors will report on the statement in their report to the shareholders.

The Sandilands report and current cost accounting

The principal features of the recommendations of the Sandilands report are:
1. Accounts should continue to be drawn up in monetary units.
2. Accounts should show the 'value to the business' of the company's assets at the balance sheet date.
3. The profit for the year should consist solely of the company's operating gains and should exclude all 'holding gains' arising from the holding of stocks and fixed assets.
4. Extraordinary gains may be shown in the profit and loss account but must be distinguished from operating gains.
5. The depreciation charge for the year is based upon the current replacement cost of the assets.
6. The holding gains should be taken to a fixed asset revaluation account and a similar process used for stock holding gains.
7. Accounts drawn up on the above basis would become the basic published accounts of the company.

The result of putting the Sandilands proposals into practice would be:
1. The asset values shown in the balance sheet would normally be by reference to their current replacement cost less depreciation based upon that value. No allowance would be made for changes in the value of net monetary assets as proposed in SSAP 7.
2. The profit and loss account would consist of a statement of:
   (a) operating gains (current cost profit), i.e., that profit struck after charging the 'value to the business' of stock used and assets owned;
   (b) extraordinary gains;
   (c) holding gains.

Holding gains should continue to be exempt from tax until they are actually realized and a deferred tax provision should be made for the ultimate liability. Tax would therefore be levied only on the CCA profits for the period. This does mean, however, that the tax on holding gains is only deferred and would become due when the company is wound up. This would make it prohibitively expensive to wind up a company and if the contention that holding gains are not profits is correct then they should not be subject to tax. Indeed, the use of the word 'gain' in holding gains is a misnomer. They are changes due to the underlying changes in the value of the monetary unit in which stock values and fixed asset values are measured.

Implementing current cost accounting measures

Fixed assets Each past year's acquisitions of fixed assets still owned by the company will have to be brought up to their value to the business at the balance sheet date and the past depreciation provision topped up to the amount appropriate for assets of their age on the revised value. Indices appropriate to the industry will normally be used for this which will be provided by the government statistical office. When the asset values have been updated in this way, the amount by which the assets are increased in value less the amount required to top up the depreciation will be taken to a fixed asset revaluation reserve. The depreciation charge for the year can then be made based upon the updated values.

Stocks and work in progress In some cases it may be possible for the company to identify the 'value to the business' of the resources consumed in respect of each individual sale. In this case the amount so derived can be used as the cost of sales and the difference between that and the historic cost treated as a holding gain.

In situations where this is not possible the cost of sales computed on a historic cost basis is adjusted in the following manner:

Price index of stock at 1 Jan.	160	
Price index of stock at 31 Dec.	220	
Therefore average price index for the year	190	
Historic cost of stocks 1 Jan.	400	
Historic cost of stocks 31 Dec.	800	
Unadjusted movement in stocks 800 − 400	=	400
Adjusted movement 691 − 475	=	216
Adjustment to cost of sales	=	184

The adjusted figures are based on using the indices to bring the opening and closing stock values to the average for the year as follows:

$$\text{Opening stock } 400 \times \frac{190}{160} = 475$$

$$\text{Closing stock } 800 \times \frac{190}{220} = 691$$

The cost of sales adjustment would reduce the profits by £184 and this would be taken to a stock revaluation reserve. Both the revaluation reserves would be adjusted by the need to provide for the deferred tax on the gains which are transferred to them and they would therefore in practice show the net of tax position.

The CCA method has the advantage of incorporating the adjustments required to deal with holding gains into the accounting process and effectively changing the generally accepted basis for preparing accounts. This can ease the transition of the tax system and changes in measuring profits for price control purposes, etc. On the other hand, the method does not take into account changes in the purchasing power of net monetary assets or liabilities. Nor are the values for different years' accounts directly comparable since they are expressed in pounds of each of the years. SSAP 7 takes into account changes in the value of net monetary assets and produces accounts which are expressed in the same unit of measure as comparable years. The supplementary statement, however, is outside the accounts proper and is less acceptable as a basis for changing tax and price control bases.

Protecting real operational profitability

Changing the method of presenting the annual financial report will not in itself affect the underlying profitability of the business. This can only be done by conscious decisions by management that will ensure that its real level of profitability is such that it can survive. The adoption of a form of inflation accounting only ensures (one hopes) that the depredations of the tax authorities are restricted to tax on real profits and that the company does not distribute dividends out of non-existent real profits. Management should consider steps which should be taken to place the company's planning and decision making on a realistic basis. This should cover such matters as:
—Pricing.
—Cost control.
—Maintaining real capital intact.
—The financing decision.
—Holding funds on an international basis.

Pricing

The restatement of the company's profits in CCA terms will sharply reduce or eliminate altogether most companies' profits as presently stated. If companies are to earn an acceptable rate of return in real terms it follows that prices of many products and services will have to be raised—a political hot potato in times of inflation. Nevertheless, if the adoption of a system of inflation accounting is to have any meaning then such adjustments will have to take place. Sandilands recognizes this by recommending that profit margins, etc., for price control purposes should be based upon CCA measurement of profit.

In practical management terms the decisions on prices should represent the cornerstone on which the company's battle against inflation is based. It is no longer viable to allow increased costs to work through the cost system before they are recognized in the form of higher prices. It is essential to set up a system to monitor the prices of the goods and services that the company uses so that the replacement cost of these can be built into product prices *now*, and not when they have worked through the costing system. The management response to input cost changes should be immediate. Remember that if inflation is 24 per cent per year, a month's delay means an adverse change in current costs of 2 per cent, which can only come out of profit margins.

If, for political reasons, prices are held down and not allowed to be adjusted for changes in the current cost of resources consumed, management must still continue to state the company's costs in current cost accounting terms in order to establish whether they should continue in business at all or to limit their trading to certain profitable sectors. The measurement of the real profit in current cost terms should also be a basis for fighting the political battle to revise prices. If this is not done there is a serious possibility for many companies that in the end the lack of real profitability will lead to their demise.

Fixed price long-term contracts should be avoided at all costs unless government or some other body is prepared to underwrite cost escalation due to inflation. It is difficult to forecast the rate of inflation one year ahead, let alone the three or four years that might be required for a major contract. It is always possible that inflation will get out of control and rapidly escalate. Until the economic and political scene becomes more settled the burden of a fixed price contract might be more than the company can bear.

Maintaining real capital intact

If a company measures its profit in CCA terms, is only taxed on that basis, and confines its distributions to shareholders to distributable profits measured on that basis, then it has gone a long way to maintaining the real capital of the company intact. The revaluation of physical assets year by year to their value to the business results not only in a restatement of asset values but the surplus arising from the revaluation adds to the value of the shareholders' funds employed in the business. There are, however, two further aspects which should be considered if the company's and the shareholders' capital are to be maintained intact in real terms. These are the effect of holding monetary assets and liabilities, and the comparability of year-by-year profits.

SSAP 7 took into account the effect of holding monetary assets and liabilities. The Sandilands CCA basis does not deal with this aspect, save to the extent that surpluses arising from the revaluation of assets accrue to the shareholders' funds. The practical effect of holding long-term liabilities is discussed later in this chapter and the discussion is confined at this stage to holding short-term assets and liabilities.

Monetary assets

Holding assets of a fixed monetary value incurs a loss in real terms during a period of inflation. For example, if customers take on average three months to pay for their purchases and inflation is running at a rate of 24 per cent per year then the company has lost 6 per cent of the sales value in real terms.

Consider a company selling a product which on 1 January costs 10p per unit and the cost of that product rises during the year at an annual rate of 24 per cent as shown in the second column below.

	Cost per unit	Sale	Number of units of stock sales proceeds could purchase
January 1	10p	1000 units at 12p = £120	1200
January 31	10·2		1177
February 28	10·4		1154
March 31	10·6		1132
April 30	10·8		1111
May 31	11·0		1091
June 30	11·2		1070
July 31	11·4		1052
August 31	11·6		1034
September 30	11·8		1017
October 31	12·0		1000

If the company sells 1000 units of its stock on 1 January at a price of 12p each, a total sales value of £120, and the cost per unit of 10·0p is in CCA terms then it has made a profit of £20 in real terms. If the company collects the cash at the time of sale it would be able to purchase 1200 units of the product with the sales proceeds, the additional 200 units of stock it could buy reflecting the profit earned. If, however, the sales proceeds are not received until the end of February, they would only be able to purchase 1154 units of stock, and, in the exceptional case of the proceeds of the sale not being received until the end of October the sales proceeds would just be able to buy the same amount of stock as was sold. In other words, holding the monetary item of debtors over 10 months would wipe out the profit on the transaction.

The narrower the profit margin the more quickly is the situation outlined above realized. If, in the previous example, the sales price had been 11p and not 12p, the profit would be wiped out if the customer did not pay until the end of May.

The losses in holding monetary assets (including cash itself) are offset to the extent that the company holds current monetary liabilities since the reverse effect applies to such items. The company gains from the decline in the real burden of the obligations. Nevertheless, in the director's armoury in the battle against inflation, the control of credit and suitable recompense for delayed payments by customers should figure prominently. If the monetary assets exceed the monetary liabilities the company sustains further losses in real terms and the purchasing power of the capital is further eroded.

Comparability

A virtue of SSAP 7 was that the previous year's profits were restated in pounds of purchasing power at the end of the current year so that if sales and/or profits for the current year are higher than those for the previous year this is an indication that sales *volume* has increased, or that real profits have increased. CCA requires no such restatement. If, for example, the company issues the following information over a series of years, it is not possible to say immediately whether the company is progressing or not. For example, if the rate of inflation is 25 per cent in each of the years 1978 and 1979 the

	1977	*1978*	*1979*
Sales (£000s)	2110	2346	2571
Operating profit (£000s)	213	232	260

values used for comparative figures in the 1978 and 1979 accounts should be increased to their value in pounds at the end of the respective years. In the 1978 accounts the values should be restated as below.

	1977 *(adjusted to* *end 1978 £s)*	*1978*
Sales (£000s)	2637	2346
Operating profit (£000s)	266	232

This shows that both sales and profits have declined in real terms from the previous year. When the 1979 accounts are produced the 1978 accounts values would need to be restated in 1979 £s (if a three-year comparison were required, the 1977 values would also need to be further restated in 1979 £s) as follows:

	1978 *(adjusted to* *end 1979 £s)*	*1979*
Sales (£000s)	2932	2571
Operating profit (£000s)	290	260

In other words, if one is making comparisons of absolute values on a year-by-year basis, *all* the values of the series should be adjusted to their value in £s or purchasing power at a single point in time, usually the last day of the latest accounting period. Only if this is done can the series of values be truly comparable. Ratios are, of course, directly comparable year by year without further adjustment, since a ratio is the comparison of two values both in £s of the same period.

When introduced, CCA should make the use of ratios a more effective management tool. The values of assets are updated each year to their value to the business in that year's pounds, and the profit measurement has excluded from normal operating profits the gains resulting from holding physical assets. As all companies are using the same basis of valuation it introduces a uniformity which makes the drawing of comparisons between companies a valid one.

Passing the burden of inflation on to others

The decline in the real burden of monetary liabilities in times of inflation is a great incentive to directors to use long-term debt as a major source of new funds. In the UK in the mid-seventies investors were willing to lend money at a negative real rate of interest. When inflation was between 25 per cent and 30 per cent on an annual basis, people and institutions were willing to lend money at 15–16 per cent. A company borrowing money at this rate of interest would incur a net of tax cost of only $7\frac{1}{2}$–8 per cent but gain the benefit of a diminution of the real value of the debt burden of 25–30 per cent both of the eventual amount to be repaid and the annual cost of interest.

If, for example, a company borrows £1 million for a 25-year period and inflation over that period is at a rate of 10 per cent per year, that £1 million in today's pounds has an equal purchasing power to £8·21 million in pounds of 25 years hence. Yet the company has only to repay £1 million of those depreciated pounds. In other words, it has been relieved of paying seven-eighths of the value it acquired. If inflation runs at a rate of 20–30 per cent per year the cost of repaying long-term debt would be negligible.

Superficially, therefore, there is a huge incentive to use long-term debt and so move the burden of inflation on to other people's shoulders. Prudent financial management dictates that other factors must be considered before one embarks upon such a policy, otherwise the long-term viability of the company might be eroded. These are:
1. The effect of the fixed burden of debt servicing if a recession is encountered in the early years after raising the loan, as discussed in chapter 9. This is reinforced by the high probability of recessionary conditions being encountered in an inflationary period. In that situation a high level of debt could be dangerous. This is illustrated by the conditions of high

inflation, high unemployment and declining volume of production in the period 1974–5.

2. The difficulty of forecasting what the rate of inflation will be over a 20-year period. In some ways inflation is a kill-or-cure disease. It contains within itself the seeds of an explosion in the rate of inflation on the German model of the 1920s. On the other hand, it can produce a reaction in society that ensures that it is brought under control. If the company commits itself to a high rate of interest for a 25-year period on the basis that the high rate of inflation will continue, but in fact inflation is brought under control, the company has loaded itself with what might prove to be an unsupportable burden of interest payments. On the other hand, if the rate of inflation explodes upwards government might be obliged to retrospectively index the capital sums borrowed, which would eliminate the benefits to be gained by borrowing.

The above illustrates the uncertainties that inflation brings into the decision-making process, not only for financial decisions, but also for many others. However, the potential gains through borrowing must receive consideration by the board. One can only advise that amounts borrowed should be well within the capacity of the company to service even if severe recessionary conditions are encountered; that the mix of debt maturities is spread over time, i.e., that they do not all mature at the same time; and that the balance between loans and shareholders' funds is appropriate for the business. Above all, the company should maintain the maximum flexibility in its future financing options.

Holding funds on an international basis

If a company trades overseas, whether directly or through a subsidiary or branch, the board should consider the implications of its holdings of cash, or debtors and creditors, in overseas currencies. One of the outcomes of inflation is likely to be changes in the rates of exchange between different countries, since it is unlikely that all countries will suffer inflation at the same rate. This is an area where expert advice should be sought, since such matters as trends in the balance of payments of various countries, problems of exchange control, and rates of interest that can be earned in different countries must all be considered. The objective of the examination of overseas trade and overseas branches and subsidiaries is to try to:

1. Ensure that cash is held in the strongest currency subject to relative interest rates, exchange control problems, etc.

2. Ensure that obligations to overseas suppliers are expressed in a weak currency rather than a strong one.

3. Ensure that sums due to the company from overseas customers are expressed in the stronger currency rather than a weak one.

Capital investment appraisal

The potential problem of inflation when dealing with capital investment projects was dealt with in the previous chapter. It only remains to emphasize that the possible distorting factors outlined on p. 174 should be carefully considered in relation to each project and if they are likely to be present then the impact of inflation on the project must be further considered.

15.
Checklist for directors

Presentation of financial reports

1. Are they presented in a manner that the laymen can understand?
2. If they are to be given to employees, is a simpler format required?
3. Have decisions been made about accounting policies to be used and have these been applied consistently?
4. Are the accounting policies properly disclosed?
5. If the company has one or more subsidiary companies, have consolidated accounts been prepared?
6. Have the requirements of the Companies Acts and SSAPs and, if appropriate, the stock exchange been observed?

The director's personal affairs vis-à-vis the company

1. Has the director any financial or other interests which may conflict with his duties to the company?
2. Has he any material interest in contracts with the company?
3. Have his interest in securities of the company and remuneration been disclosed?

Books of account

1. Have proper books of account been kept?
2. Are there adequate records of:
   (a) receipts and payments?
   (b) sales and purchases?
   (c) assets and liabilities?
3. Are there adequate records of stocks, etc?

Taxation

1. (a) Have adequate steps been taken to ensure that the tax implications of decisions are incorporated into the decision-making process?
2. Is the company a close company?
3. For close companies:

(a) have the possible implications of apportionment been taken into account in framing the dividend policy?
(b) should the company's earnings be distributed as additional directors' remuneration?
(c) are the assets used in the business in the most appropriate ownership?

Relations with the company's bankers

1. Has a strategy been devised for keeping the bank fully appraised of the company's activities?
2. When seeking bank facilities have the board defined:
   (a) why the extra funds are required?
   (b) how the borrowing is to be repaid?
   (c) security for the loan?
   (d) other supporting information?

Trade credit

1. Is the company making the optimum use of trade credit, i.e., obtaining maximum cash discounts while taking the overall longest payment period consistent with liquidity and other constraints?
2. If the company has major creditors is it appropriate to use credit insurance?

Dividends

1. Are there available realized profits from which a proposed dividend can be paid?
2. Is it properly authorized by the board?
3. Has a consistent policy for dividends been adopted by the board?
4. Have the requirements of the company's articles of association been satisfied?
5. Is the company's cash position sufficiently strong to support the payments?
6. Has consideration been given to using small scrip issues instead of cash dividends?

Raising new capital

1. Have the effects on return on shareholders' funds of using the available sources been considered?
2. Have the implications for the risk of business failure been considered?
3. Where it is proposed to use debt:
   (a) will it leave a margin of debt capacity available for future financing needs if required?
   (b) are the likely cash flows, both for normal years and years of recession, adequate to service the proposed total debt?
   (c) is there any bunching in the pattern of debt maturities?

4. Rights issues:
   (a) is there sufficient unissued authorized share capital to cover the issue?
   (b) is the proposed issue price too high in relation to the present market price of the shares?
   (c) are profits likely to expand sufficiently to maintain the shareholders' values?
5. Will the proposed funding operation affect the control of the company?

Interpreting financial results

1. Are the appropriate historical ratios reported to the board?
2. Can operating ratios be useful to control and if so should the company join an inter-firm comparison group?
3. Can intra-company comparisons be used within the company?
4. Are the reasons for changes in the ratios analysed and explained?

Planning for growth

1. Are the directors committed to long-term planning?
2. Is there an adequate system for monitoring and forecasting changes in the environment?
3. Is there adequate communication between research and development and marketing so that needs and opportunities are quickly identified?
4. Is there a formal organization for long-term planning?
5. Are long-term plans regularly reviewed?
6. Has the appropriate planning period been adopted?
7. Are the corporate objectives defined?
8. Are proposed strategies adequately tested against required profits?
9. Have individual manager objectives been reconciled with the corporate objectives?

Planning for survival

1. Is the company overtrading?
2. Is there the right balance between long-term and short-term assets and liabilities?
3. Does the board know how much is to be spent on fixed investment in each of the next three to five years?
4. Has provision been made to finance those levels of fixed investment with long-term funds?
5. Is there an adequate system for controlling the credit given to customers?
6. Is there an adequate system for controlling the investment of funds in stocks and work in progress?

Operational planning and control

1. Do the proposed budgets facilitate the achievement of the long-term objectives?

2. Do the directors themselves plan and control through the corporate planning and control systems?
3. Is there adequate information on which to base plans?
4. Are managers sufficiently involved in and committed to the planning process?
5. Do the budgets represent an adequate measure of manager performance?
6. Are reports timely?
7. Have the directors made a critical review of the proposed budgets?
8. Do the directors know:
   (a) what sales are expected for each product?
   (b) what expenditure can be incurred by each manager?
   (c) what profit should be generated at each profit centre?
   (d) what movements are expected in fixed asset investment and in working capital elements?
   (e) individual product or service costs?

Cash planning and control
1. What is the planned cash position period-by-period during the year?
2. Are identified cash deficiencies covered by bank or other borrowing?
3. Is the current cash position compared with budget reported to the board?
4. Are events which might affect future cash flows reported?
5. How do the ratios computed from the balance sheet at the end of the budget period and the operating budget compare with those of previous years?
6. What are the reasons for changes?

Decision taking
1. Is the constraint on the company the ability to sell or is there some physical or other constraint on the level of activity?
2. Are changes from one state to the other identified and reported?
3. Have the board established appropriate strategies for:
   (a) volume and capacity?
   (b) assessing relative profitability of products, etc?
   (c) pricing in conditions of spare capacity?
   (d) direction of marketing effort?
   (e) selecting the optimum product range where there are constraints on volume?

Planning and appraising long-term investment
1. Is each year's mix of projects in conformity with the long-term objectives?
2. Do they provide an adequate pattern of profit and cash flows?
3. Have the directors established the financial criteria for the appraisal method?

4. Is there a proper organizational framework for the preparation, submission and approval of projects?
5. Have the assumptions on which project cash flows are based been adequately tested?
6. Have alternative ways of achieving the objective of the investments been investigated?
7. Is there a post audit of projects?
8. Are directors aware of the accuracy of the forecasting used in the presentation of projects?
9. Where appropriate, have projects been subjected to probability and/or sensitivity tests?

Combating inflation
1. Do the company's financial reports separate the holding gains for stocks, work in progress and fixed assets from operating gains?
2. Are increases in operating costs reported as soon as they are identified?
3. Are prices adjusted for cost increases as soon as they are identified?
4. Is the company minimizing its holding of monetary assets?
5. Should the company use long-term debt to ease the burden of inflation?
6. In capital investment appraisal:
   (a) are elements of cost inflating at rates different from the general rate of inflation? If so, how significant are they in relation to the value of the investment?
   (b) are there obstacles to adjusting prices to cost changes?
7. Where the answer to 6 (a) and (b) are positive, have special methods of forecasting cash flows in pounds of current purchasing power in each of the years been used?
8. Are funds held on an international basis held in the right currency?
9. Are obligations to and from overseas suppliers and customers expressed in the right currency?

Index

Printed in Great Britain
at the Alden Press, Oxford